Advance Praise for
YOU HAVE THE RIGHT TO REMAIN INNOCENT

"In this quick and wonderful read, one of America's most eloquent writers on legal subjects makes clear why you should never, ever answer police questions about your past conduct, however virtuous and civic-minded you may be. *You Have the Right to Remain Innocent* describes a stream of miscarriages of justice that occurred only because innocent suspects cooperated with deceptive officers preying on their ignorance and good intentions. The book makes its case with verve and passion, and even if you are a tough-on-crime conservative or a police chief, it is likely to persuade you."

—Albert W. Alschuler, University of Chicago Law School,
former federal prosecutor

"James Duane is an experienced criminal defense lawyer and a tough-minded legal scholar. This is not just a book of advice; it is a passionate and disturbing critique of the rules governing police interrogations in the United States. It repays careful reading."

—David Alan Sklansky, Stanford Law School,
former federal prosecutor

"The stories in *You Have the Right to Remain Innocent* will help you remember *why* you should not talk to the police and exactly *how* to assert your rights. This book could save you—or your children—years of imprisonment for a crime committed by someone else. Read it and then make sure your kids read it too."

—Randy E. Barnett, Georgetown University Law Center, director of the Georgetown Center for the Constitution

"James Duane's amazing but true stories of innocent people exonerated after decades of wrongful imprisonment (which could have been avoided if they had just insisted on their fundamental right to avoid self-incrimination) are riveting reminders of the high price we pay, as individuals and as a society, when we fail to assert our constitutional rights."

—Laurence H. Tribe, Harvard Law School

YOU HAVE
THE RIGHT
TO REMAIN
INNOCENT

YOU HAVE THE RIGHT TO REMAIN INNOCENT

What Police Officers Tell Their Children
about the Fifth Amendment

JAMES DUANE

Little
a

Published by Little A, New York
www.apub.com

Amazon, the Amazon logo, and Little A are trademarks of Amazon.com, Inc., or its affiliates.

ISBN-13: 9781503933392
ISBN-10: 1503933393

Cover design by Tim Green, Faceout Studio

Printed in the United States of America

Dedicated with love to my sons,
Daniel and Solomon.

CONTENTS

YOU HAVE
THE RIGHT
TO REMAIN
INNOCENT

I

DON'T TALK TO POLICE

[A]ny lawyer worth his salt will tell the suspect in no uncertain terms to make no statement to the police under any circumstances.

—Former United States Attorney General and Supreme Court Justice Robert Jackson, *Watts v. Indiana*, 338 U.S. 49, 59 (1949) (concurring opinion)

In the past five years, I have spoken dozens of times to thousands of individuals around the United States about the right to remain silent. Most of my audience members have been students in college or law school. Everywhere I go, I just about always make a point to ask how many people in attendance have a parent who is a police officer or a prosecutor—and of those attendees, what their parents have advised them about the Fifth Amendment. In almost every group, there is at least one student who tells me that his father is a state trooper, or that her mother is a prosecutor. Every time this happens, without exception, the student in question has told me basically the same thing: "Years ago, my parents explained to me that if I were ever approached by a law enforcement officer, I was to call them immediately, and they made sure that I would never agree to talk to the police." (Most of these young people also volunteered that their parents in law enforcement advised them to never allow an officer to search their apartment or car, but that is the subject for another book.) Not once have I met the child of a member of law enforcement who had been told anything different.

Everyone who is privileged enough to know how the criminal justice system operates in America would never advise their loved ones to waive the right to remain silent in the face of a criminal investigation. We routinely see people in power, such as police officers and government officials, pleading the fifth (like Lois Lerner, the former director of the Internal Revenue Service's Exempt Organizations unit, who asserted her Fifth Amendment privilege and refused to answer any questions when she was summoned before a congressional committee in 2013).[1] These are officials who have made a career out of talking people into waiving their right to remain silent, but when the questions are suddenly directed at them, they will not waive their own.

You need to pause for a moment and let that sink in.

It doesn't matter whether you are a liberal or conservative. I do not even care whether you are heartless enough to remain unconcerned about the fact that our legal system routinely convicts innocent people. Nobody of sound mind can dispute that there is something fundamentally wrong, and intrinsically corrupt, about a legal system that encourages police officers and prosecutors to do everything in their power to persuade you and your children (no matter how young or old) to "do the right thing" and talk—when they tell their own children the exact opposite.

I intend to bring to an end, once and for all, that obscene double standard in the American criminal justice system that allows only the citizens who are in the know to protect themselves from a legal system that is designed to prey upon ignorance and good intentions. Most people have no idea what they are up against when they agree to talk to the police. Everybody in this country faces a terrible risk, however small, that someday the police will come calling. Someday, you might even be arrested and asked whether you would mind answering just a few questions to "help clear things up." You have no way to know whether that fateful moment will ever come your way, or when it will happen. But if it does happen to you, or perhaps to one of your children, it will come without warning and you will suddenly have to make one of the most important decisions of your life. You will almost certainly *not* be offered the chance to speak to anyone other than the officer. The only advice you will receive in that moment is likely to come straight from the police officer, who will lie to you by claiming to represent your best interests. And the police will make these claims very convincingly, because they have been practicing the same lies on other people for years. In that moment, if you make the wrong decision, or if you simply don't know any better, what you say could cost you your freedom, perhaps for the rest of your life.

***

This book will explain what every police officer knows about the American criminal justice system. It will explain how even innocent criminal suspects can unwittingly give the police information that can be used to help convict them of a crime they did not commit. I am not claiming, of course, that it is *never* a good idea to talk to the police. A few years ago, I recorded a lecture about the importance of the Fifth Amendment and some of the reasons why you should never agree to answer unexpected and unsolicited questions from the police. That video has been viewed millions of times on YouTube, which is a great thing for the country. As a result, my mailbox has been filled ever since by comments and questions, many from those who wonder whether I mean that one should avoid speaking to police in every imaginable scenario. Of course not. That would be ridiculous.

Let me quickly clarify and acknowledge that there are several situations in which it is perfectly fine to talk briefly to the police. For example, you might get locked out of your own house and find you have to climb into your darkened home in the middle of the night through a window, perhaps by breaking the glass. Or maybe you have some strange reason for standing outside at night and looking through the windows of your home with a flashlight or for jimmying the lock of your car. Or perhaps you have some lawful reason to be walking around in the middle of the night inside a government building that has been locked up, one which nobody else has any reason to be inside. Or you're a teenager with an innocent explanation for walking down an alley carrying two brand-new bikes while everyone else your age is in school. These are all reasonably suspicious activities.

If a police officer encounters you in one of those moments, he or she has every right to ask you two simple questions. Memorize these two questions so you will not be tempted to answer any others:

> Who are you?
> What are you doing *right here, right now*?

If you are ever approached by a police officer with those two questions, and your God-given common sense tells you that the officer is being reasonable in asking for an explanation, don't be a jerk. Even if you are angry and frustrated about being locked out of your house, try to see this from the police's point of view. They are only looking out for your best interests. Would you want them to ask those same questions of any other individual caught breaking in through one of your windows, or watching your family? Of course you would. If you have an innocent explanation for your presence at that time and in that place, tell the police about it. Tell them that it is your own house. Or tell them that you are in an empty courthouse in the middle of the night because you work there, and show them your identification. They will appreciate your cooperation, and that will be the end of it. If you unreasonably refuse to answer those two questions, they might put you under arrest, and I would not blame them.

I am not a member of a racial minority, and I am well aware of the reality that far too many individuals of color are harassed by officers for no good reason, so it is easier for me to give the above advice than for others who have been subject to such harassment. After all, I have never been stopped by a police officer who thought I was riding a bike that looked like it might be too expensive for somebody of *my* race. And I cannot imagine how frustrating such prejudicial suspicion must be.

But you cannot make your situation any better by refusing to cooperate with the officer, no matter how unreasonable you may think the police officer is being, or by refusing to disclose two simple things: (1) your name, and (2) whether you have some lawful reason for your curious presence or conduct at that moment at some place *where the officer already knows you are*, because he or she is standing right there with you.

Those are the only two things you should tell the police officer in that context, and they are both *in the present tense*. (You might as well cooperate with such a request, by the way, because the Fifth Amendment does not normally give you the right to refuse to tell the police your name anyway.[2]) That is it. But if the police officer tries to strike up a conversation with you about the *past*, and where you were thirty minutes earlier, and who you were with, and where you had dinner, and with whom—you will not answer those questions. You will not be rude, but you will always firmly decline, with all due respect, to answer those questions.[3]

***

Everybody in this country owes a deep debt of gratitude to law enforcement officers. Many of them take great personal risks every day for our protection. All of us depend on them heavily, more than most of us appreciate, for the defense and protection of our lives, our property, and our most cherished liberties. I thank God for the unselfishness and the bravery of police officers, and not one word in this book should be taken to imply otherwise.

So then why do I say that you should almost never talk to the police when they come to you with questions about your past? They are not generally any more dishonest than most individuals you will deal with. Of course, we all know that the worst officers (just like the worst defense attorneys, in my line of work) are sometimes caught red handed and convicted of terrible crimes, maybe involving fraud and deception. But I'm not writing about those police officers. If you ever fall into the hands of a police officer so corrupt that the officer would intentionally lie in order to cause undeserved legal trouble for you, there is unfortunately nothing you can do to completely protect yourself from that risk. (Although even in that case, as you will see, your odds of staying out of trouble will be better if you keep your mouth shut, because you will make it a little harder for the officer to successfully lie about what you said.)

No, the advice contained in this book—the same advice that police officers give their own children—is not based on any assumptions or suspicions about the overall morality of police officers. It is based on two simple but unavoidable facts about every police officer, including the most noble and virtuous. The only two problems I have with the police (although they are very big problems) are these:

The first problem with the police is that they are only human. They cannot know everything. For instance, when confronted with opposing accounts of the same situation, they cannot know who is really telling them the truth. And because they are only human, police officers, just like all of us, do not like to be embarrassed by admitting that they made some sort of a mistake, especially if it concerns a matter so serious that it might lead to them being sued. They do not even like to admit it to themselves. That is why police officers, like all humans, are subject to a powerful phenomenon that psychologists call *confirmation bias*. This means that after they have come to a conclusion, especially if it is a conclusion that they have publicly announced (for example, by arresting someone and accusing him of a serious crime), it is very difficult for them to admit that perhaps they have made a terrible mistake. It is much easier and more comfortable for them to convince themselves that they did not make a mistake, and that their initial accusations were correct. Their memories will gladly cooperate in that effort. Even if they are not aware of how it is happening, they might recall nonexistent details to coincide with and corroborate the story they have already begun persuading themselves to believe.

Just like the rest of us, police are frustrated by important and difficult questions for which there are no discernable answers. And, just like us, they love the powerful psychological satisfaction that comes from convincing themselves that in fact the riddle has been solved. When a terrible crime is committed, every human being with a heart desperately wants to believe that we can find the offender. And if there is only one suspect available to us, most of us are surprisingly good at convincing ourselves that maybe he or she really is the one to blame, and that perhaps the circumstantial evidence against him or her is fairly powerful after all.

But the fact that police officers are "only human" is only one of the two problems. The other problem is that they are working within a legal system that is highly imperfect. That is not their fault, because they did not design the system. But as this book will demonstrate, it is a broken system that relies heavily on the judgment of judges and juries who are also only human, and who can sometimes be unduly influenced by irrational prejudices and assumptions. They make mistakes too. And judges, for many years, have given police officers encouragement and incentives to engage in all sorts of extraordinary deception when they are interviewing criminal suspects. They receive sophisticated training at the police academy in methods of interrogation that are remarkably successful in getting guilty people to make confessions and incriminating statements.[4] You cannot blame them for using such methods—after all, we all agree that guilty people (at least the dangerous ones) ought to be caught and put behind bars—but the problem is that these methods of calculated deception are *too* effective. *They do not merely work on the guilty.* At least some of these methods, it turns out, have proven to be just as effective in getting *innocent* people to make incriminating statements, and sometimes even outright confessions.

Do not think for a minute that you can trust a police officer who *seems* to be open minded and undecided about whether he will arrest you after you are finished with an "interview"—the police are *trained* to act that way, to get you to talk with them for many hours until you finally give up in exhaustion. The most recent and comprehensive investigation, which took a careful look at 250 prisoners exonerated by DNA evidence, found that 16 percent of them made what's called a *false confession*: admitting their commission of a crime that they did not commit.[5] Those are the cases in which the defendant actually confessed; in many more cases, the innocent suspect denied all guilt, sometimes for hours, but still gave the police a statement that was then used to help convict him. Out of all the hundreds of innocent men and women who were wrongly convicted but later exonerated by DNA evidence, more than 25 percent made either a false confession or an incriminating statement.[6] Every one of those suspects would have been much better off, and might have avoided going to prison altogether, if they had simply read this book.

***

Many years ago, when the world was much simpler than it is today, a young legal advisor named Jiminy Cricket was able to cheerfully and enthusiastically advise Pinocchio, "Always let your conscience be your guide!" It was not terrible advice at the time, because in those days there was a fairly close correspondence between law and morality. In those days, nothing was forbidden by the law unless it was obviously immoral, dishonest, or dangerous to the general public. It was almost inconceivable that an accused criminal could ever claim to have no idea that whatever he or she was doing was against the law.

Those days are long gone. Because of the matrix of rampant horrors often described as *overcriminalization*, it is no longer possible for you to rely on your own conscience or common sense as a reliable guide for whether you have committed a crime. One recent investigation revealed that the United States Congress was passing a new criminal law once a week on average.[7] It has been reported that the problem is so severe that even the Congressional Research Service is no longer able to keep count of the exact number of federal crimes![8] These laws are scattered throughout all the sections of the United States Code and include thousands of criminal statutes. Even if you somehow had the time to read every page of the federal laws written down in the United States Code—and even practicing lawyers no longer have the time to read all those laws—you still would not know all the different ways you could be prosecuted by the federal government. That's because many of those statutes written by Congress reference the obscure provisions of many thousands of regulations that have been issued by every federal regulatory agency. It has been estimated that there are tens of thousands of these obscure regulations, any one of which could potentially subject you to criminal prosecution.[9] And that is just the list of federal criminal statutes; the states have an even greater number of crimes on the books.

As Justice Stephen Breyer of the United States Supreme Court correctly complained in 1998, "The complexity of modern federal criminal law, codified in several thousand sections of the United States Code and the virtually infinite variety of factual circumstances that might trigger an investigation into a possible violation of the law, make it difficult for anyone to know, in advance, just when a particular set of statements might later appear (to a prosecutor) to be relevant to some such investigation."[10] In other words: the deck is stacked heavily against you, and you have no idea what you are up against.

People who want to read all the federal laws on the books, if they had three decades of free time on their hands, could find them all at any law library collected in a voluminous set of books called the *United States Code*, which is organized in different sections called *titles*. One of those fifty-two sections, known as Title 18, is called "Crimes and Criminal Procedure." It is where any ordinary American citizen would expect to find a complete list of all the crimes recognized under federal law. But even if you took years of your life to read through that entire portion of the Code, believe it or not, you would have missed hundreds of the criminal laws on the books, because they are not all contained in Title 18! Why not? There is not one good reason. It is almost as if our government was determined to do whatever it could to make it nearly impossible for the average American to have any idea what is and what is not forbidden by the law. Legend has it that one wicked Roman emperor had his laws posted on the top of a high pillar so that no citizen could find and read them, but at least you could get at them with a ladder.

The thousands of American criminal statutes no longer coincide with common sense. Years ago, the Supreme Court held that you can be convicted and imprisoned for committing a crime even if you had no criminal intent and absolutely no knowledge that your conduct was forbidden by any law. Congress has exploited that loophole with ruthless impunity and has passed countless laws that do not require the prosecutor to show that you had any idea that your conduct might be illegal. Former United States Attorney General Edwin Meese has noted that the average American has "little or no hope of knowing all of the thousands of criminal-law statutes—and tens of thousands of criminal-law regulations—by which they must abide in order to remain on the right side of the law. This is one of the primary reasons why it is no longer possible to avoid becoming a criminal by relying on one's conscience and general understanding of the law."[11] As he has correctly complained, Congress and the state legislatures have created thousands of exotic crimes that "serve as snares and traps for the average American," and which "transform activities that until recently no one ever considered criminal—such as erecting a fence around your property, investing for your retirement, or disposing of used cooking oil—into potentially criminal conduct."[12]

Here are just a few examples of this madness. It is a federal criminal offense to wear or display the emblem of the 4-H clubs, or even just a "colorable imitation," if you are trying to fool anyone into thinking that you are associated with those clubs with the intent to defraud that person, and you may be sent to prison for up to six months for that violation.[13] You can also go to prison for up to six months for the unauthorized use of the character or the name *Woodsy Owl* for the purpose of making a profit.[14] The same is also true if you knowingly possess any alligator grass or water chestnut or hyacinth plants that have been shipped across state lines, or just the *seeds* of such grass or plants, even if you were not the one who sent or received them when they crossed state lines.[15] (In fact, you can also be sent to prison—even if you played no part in that supposedly dangerous shipment—if all you did was *advertise* your willingness to do such a dangerous thing.) It is also a federal offense, again carrying a potential penalty of up to six months in a federal prison, if you use the Swiss coat of arms in any advertising for your business.[16] I would include a picture of that coat of arms here so you could see what I am talking about, but I cannot take the chance that I might be sent to prison. Two years ago, young sailors thought they were doing a good deed by freeing a five-hundred-pound sea turtle who had become entangled in a buoy line that wrapped around its head and fins, but they were later told by an agent from the National Oceanic and Atmospheric Administration that what they did was a violation of the Endangered Species Act, which makes it illegal to handle an endangered or protected species.[17] Luckily for them, they were members of the Kennedy family, so they were not prosecuted. But they could have been, and their good intentions and their ignorance of this law would have been no defense at all.[18]

To make matters worse, the statutes themselves are carelessly and clumsily crafted. For far too long, Congress and the state legislatures have been filled with men and women who are either unable or unwilling to write laws with the care and precision necessary to make them plain and unambiguous. It takes a lot of time and hard work to carefully draft a criminal law so that it is directed specifically at the kind of misconduct that Congress means to forbid. It is so much easier to write the statute as broadly as possible and let the courts try to sort out the mess. Just take a look at these horrendous examples.

One federal law makes it a crime "to import, export, transport, sell, receive, acquire, or purchase any *fish or wildlife or plant* taken, possessed, transported, or sold in violation of any *law, treaty, or regulation* of the *United States* or in violation of any *Indian tribal law* [or] . . . any law or regulation of *any State* or in violation of *any foreign law*."[19] This single sentence, one of many thousands contained in the United States Code, incorporates by reference the crimes set forth in the laws of every other country in the world, and applies to every sort of animal, fish, or plant. People have been prosecuted and convicted under this law for possessing a lobster or a fish—even though the possession of that creature did not violate any other American law—just because it was imported from another country that *did* forbid such possession. Did you know that you could be guilty of a felony under federal law if you are found in possession of a "short lobster," because it was a little smaller than one you could lawfully possess?[20] If you are charged with such an offense, it does not matter whether it was dead or alive, or whether you killed it; it does not even matter whether you killed it in self-defense. You will not find this law even if you set aside five years of your life to read the entire section of the United States Code governing "Crimes and Criminal Procedure," however, because this crime is listed in Title 16 (sec. 1857) of the United States Code, in a section that collects all the laws governing the subject of "Conservation."

Another federal law makes it a felony for any person "knowingly to deliver or cause to be delivered for transmission through the mails or interstate commerce by *telegraph, telephone, wireless, or other means* of communication *false or misleading* or knowingly inaccurate reports *concerning crop or market information or conditions* that affect or tend to affect the price of any commodity in interstate commerce."[21] For this "crime," you can be fined up to one million dollars and imprisoned for up to ten years. If you are ever prosecuted for a violation of this law, the way it is written, all the government needs to do to put you behind bars is to prove that you sent anybody a single bit of inaccurate information that somehow concerned crop or commodity market information or conditions. It does not matter whether you sent that message by telephone or mail or telegraph. It does not matter who you sent that letter to. It does not matter whether the information was actually false, or merely misleading. It does not matter whether your note actually had any effect on market prices anywhere, or even whether you intended for it to have that effect. The way this law was written by the morons in Congress, you are guilty of a felony if you send a postcard to your grandmother in a nursing home, trying to make her feel better by lying about how nice the weather has been in Florida, or how low the gas prices have been. And you will not find this law in Title 18 either; this one is buried in the bowels of Title 7 (sec. 13), which lists the laws supposedly regulating "Agriculture."

Even criminal laws that are aimed at truly harmful conduct are almost always ridiculously overbroad. One asinine federal law on the books has the perfectly natural objective of trying to prevent terrorists from using chemical weapons to cause the massive infliction of death or physical injury on huge numbers of innocent persons. But the way it is actually written, it forbids anyone to use or merely "possess" any "chemical weapon," which is defined to include "any chemical which through its chemical action on life processes can cause death, *temporary incapacitation* or permanent harm to persons *or animals*," unless it is used for certain—very narrowly defined—purposes permitted under the law.[22] The potential for temporary inconvenience or mild irritation to a single animal would classify a substance as a chemical weapon. The way this statute is written, as the Supreme Court noted with frustration a couple years ago in *Bond v. United States*, it is a felony under federal law if a parent, "exasperated by the children's repeated failure to clean the goldfish tank, . . . considers poisoning the fish with a few drops of vinegar."[23] And of course that is only half the problem, because this statute forbids both the use and the mere *possession* of such a chemical weapon, so you would be guilty of a violation just by picking up the vinegar at the grocery store for that purpose, even if federal agents caught and arrested you before you poisoned the tank.

The same is often true of the clumsy laws written by state legislatures. In my home state of Virginia, it is a crime to "hunt, trap, take, capture, kill, attempt to take, capture or kill, *possess*, deliver for transportation, transport, cause to be transported, by any means whatever, receive for transportation or export, or import, at any time or in any manner, *any wild bird or wild animal or the carcass or any part thereof*, except as specifically permitted by law."[24] Once again, we have a law that is aimed at a sensible purpose—controlling the illegal and unrestricted killing and possession of certain wild animals, like deer or bears, without the proper authorization and licenses—but the idiots who wrote it could not go to the trouble of writing it narrowly enough so that it would be limited to its intended purpose. The way this absurd law is written, you are guilty of a crime as long as you merely "possess" any "part" of anything that was once a wild bird or animal. That would include a sand dollar or a seashell that you picked up on the beach, or a necklace your granddaughter bought you in the Bahamas with a shark tooth in it. A few years ago, a newly elected member of the Virginia legislature was told by security at the state capitol that he was violating this law because he'd brought a pair of deer antlers to hang on his wall; even though neither he nor anyone else had killed or injured those deer, since the antlers had been naturally shed on his property, he was guilty of a crime under Virginia law.[25]

Because of laws like these and countless others, legal experts now agree that just about everybody in the nation, whether they know it or not, is guilty of numerous felonies for which they could be prosecuted. One reliable estimate is that the average American now commits approximately three felonies a day.[26] As one federal judge recently observed, because there are "thousands of federal crimes and hundreds of thousands of federal regulations that can be criminally enforced," the sad truth today is that "most people have committed at least one crime carrying serious consequences," including countless Americans who have no idea what law they have broken, or how they may have done so.[27] That is why you cannot listen to your conscience when faced by a police officer and think, *I have nothing to hide.*

Many prosecutors and other cynical observers who read this book will dismiss my complaint, and insist that there is no reason to fear the ludicrous breadth of America's criminal statutes. There is no need for alarm, they will assure us, because we can all safely trust in the good faith of America's prosecutors and their discretion to not hassle you or seek to imprison you for innocent and harmless conduct, even if it does happen to be technically forbidden by some obscure statute. But there have been many confirmed cases of federal agents and prosecutors who proved that they cannot be trusted to exercise such restraint—either because they had too much time on their hands, or perhaps subscribed to a corrupt political agenda, or maybe just got a kick out of what they thought was their own ingenuity in exploiting the language of some badly written law to prosecute someone.[28]

Just a few years ago, for example, the United States Department of Justice actually used the federal chemical weapons ban to prosecute a woman for putting a mild chemical irritant on the mailbox of her husband's girlfriend, even though nobody was even seriously, much less permanently, injured.[29] The victim of this attack suffered nothing more than a minor thumb burn that was readily treated by rinsing with water. That was the same case in which the Supreme Court of the United States unanimously concluded that, if they adhered to the insane interpretation of this terrible statute that was being defended by the Department of Justice, you could be prosecuted for using a few drops of vinegar to poison your child's goldfish. The Supreme Court correctly noted that the government's proposed interpretation of this law "would sweep in everything from the detergent under the kitchen sink to the stain remover in the laundry room."[30] Luckily for the defendant, the Supreme Court said it would not agree to "transform a statute passed to implement the international Convention on Chemical Weapons into one that also makes it a federal offense to poison goldfish."[31] The late justice of the Supreme Court Antonin Scalia correctly described that federal law as "a statute that should be the envy of every lawmaker bent on trapping the unwary with vague and uncertain criminal prohibitions."[32]

And this sort of thing happens all the time. Even more recently, the Supreme Court once again had to reverse the Obama administration, this time for prosecuting a man who threw some fish over the side of his boat. John Yates, a commercial fisherman, reportedly caught six dozen undersized red grouper in federal waters in the Gulf of Mexico, and allegedly threw them into the sea to prevent federal authorities from confirming that he had done so.[33] Incredibly, he was then prosecuted for a violation of the Sarbanes-Oxley Act, a federal statute that had been written and passed to protect financial investors and restore trust in financial markets following the collapse of Enron Corporation by forbidding corporate and accounting deception and cover-ups. Congress had made it a federal crime, punishable by up to twenty years in prison, for anyone to alter, destroy, conceal, or cover up "any record, document, or tangible object" to obstruct any governmental investigation. Even though it was undisputed that the law was concerned with corporate document shredding and destruction to hide evidence of financial wrongdoing, the Justice Department pointed out that the incredibly overbroad statute actually referred to any "tangible object," which would technically include a few fish. The Supreme Court overturned that conviction, holding that it was an unreasonable interpretation of this unreasonably broad statute. Although a few justices on the court would have upheld that conviction, even they agreed that the statute was "a bad law—too broad and undifferentiated, with too-high maximum penalties, which give prosecutors too much leverage and sentencers too much discretion."[34] They wrote that the statute in this respect "is unfortunately not an outlier, but an emblem of a deeper pathology in the federal criminal code," which they called the problem of "overcriminalization and excessive punishment in the U.S. Code."[35]

The defendants in those cases were two of the lucky ones, because they were ultimately vindicated by the highest court in the land—but not until after they had been forced to undergo years of anxiety and great expense in defending themselves against ridiculous charges that never should have been filed. In both cases, the defendants lost all of their arguments in the lower federal courts. The Supreme Court justices are able to decide fewer than 1 percent of all the appeals that are presented to them to consider, so it would be madness to imagine that the Supreme Court could ever be counted upon to keep the problem under control.

The monstrous potential for injustice created by this modern farce has become, quite by accident, the most important reason why the Fifth Amendment is now more precious than ever before. Even in this modern age, there are many ignorant sentimentalists who believe that our government is deserving of our loyal cooperation and support, and that every good patriot with an innocent conscience should be glad to answer any questions from government agents. That is hogwash. Perhaps it was true a century ago—I deeply regret that it is no longer true—but the United States criminal justice system long ago lost any legitimate claim to the loyal cooperation of American citizens. You cannot write tens of thousands of criminal statutes, including many touching upon conduct that is neither immoral nor dangerous, write those laws as broadly as you can imagine, scatter them throughout the thousands of pages of the United States Code—and then expect decent, law-abiding, unsuspecting citizens to cooperate with an investigation into whether they may have violated some law they have never even heard about. The next time some police officer or government agent asks you whether you would be willing to answer a few questions about where you have been and what you have been doing, you must respectfully but very firmly decline.

***

One of the worst things about talking to the police, as we will see, is the fact that our legal system permits and even encourages the police to lie to you in ways that are absolutely shocking, and to use all sorts of grotesque deceptions if that is what it takes to get you to waive your right to remain silent. The police are well aware that many of us harbor the mistaken assumption that they are even our "friends." But the truth is that you cannot safely trust a single thing police officers say when they are trying to get you to answer their questions.

I am not claiming that police officers are, by and large, generally dishonest individuals. I am not saying anything about their personality or their general morality. Certainly there are some who are less honest than most, but that is probably no more true in policing than it is in other professions. Then why do I say that you cannot believe one word of what they tell you? Because the police are only doing what they were trained to do, and what they are constantly encouraged to do by the courts. They are only following orders, because that is the way our corrupt legal system is designed to work.

Far too many ignorant American citizens naturally assume that there must be some kind of legal oversight of police interrogations. After all, we all know that car salespeople and even shoe salespeople are obligated to be straight with you when they are trying to enter into a transaction involving only money, and they can be prosecuted or sued if they are caught using intentional deception to defraud you into giving up a mere twenty dollars. So it stands to reason, innocent people frequently assume, that there must be some similar rules restricting the ability of the police to trick you into giving up your most precious constitutional rights. I would not blame you for thinking such a thing, but you would be dead wrong.

The rampant use of dishonesty and deception by the police is a serious threat to the administration of justice in two different ways. First of all, it is of course one of the most powerful ways to persuade even innocent people to make a false confession, as we shall see. But it also has a more insidious effect as well, because even if the police do not use deception to persuade you to make an outright confession, they might persuade you to give them a little bit of information that can later be used against you in front of a jury.

Many years ago, when the Supreme Court of the United States was much more liberal than it is today, it stated that there are certain forms of police deception so extreme that they are over the line and might be cause for preventing the police from using against you anything you said after you were so deceived.[36] But the Supreme Court never clearly defined what those limits might be and has largely left it to the lower courts to work out how much police dishonesty is "too much" and would preclude the courts from using your admissions against you. And since those vague constitutional protections have been largely left in the hands of the lower courts, they have been so severely watered down that police officers can lie to you concerning just about every aspect of the investigation, and do so without corrupting the admissibility of your testimony.

They will lie to you about what crime they are actually investigating, whether they regard you as a suspect, whether they plan to prosecute you, what evidence they have against you, whether your answers may help you, whether your statements are off the record, and whether the other witnesses have agreed to talk to them—even about what those witnesses have or have not said.[37] That is just a partial list. The bottom line is plain: you cannot safely trust a single word that you hear from the mouth of a police officer who is trying to get you to talk. The police may even lie to you about whether your loved ones are dead or alive: In 2004, Illinois police officers called to investigate the disappearance of a three-year-old girl mistakenly thought her father might be a suspect. Under the pretense that they were looking for the parents' help in locating the girl, they invited the parents to the station and questioned them for an hour before they finally told the parents that her dead body had *already* been found, even before they asked the parents to come down to the station.[38] If you are being questioned by the police and trying to decide what your next move ought to be, you need to proceed on the assumption that everything you think you know about the investigation is a lie, and that you know absolutely *nothing* for sure about what is going on outside that room.

Let me give you a few examples of how easily the police can use outrageous forms of deception to get almost anyone, including innocent people, to make an outright confession—or at least to give the police a statement that can be used to help convict them. In 2008, just two days after her infant son suffocated, Nga Truong, a sixteen-year-old girl, was interrogated for two hours by police officers.[39] She was young and unusually vulnerable, having recently experienced both the birth and the death of her infant son. At first, like most innocent people, she denied her guilt repeatedly. And the police officers, as it turned out, actually had no evidence that anyone had killed her child, or that his death was the result of anything other than natural causes. But the officers aggressively questioned her for hours, intentionally misrepresenting that they could prove someone had killed him and she had probably done it.

In an effort to break her down and talk her into admitting that she had smothered her son, the police lied to her and told her that they wanted to "help her," and that if she confessed, they would keep her case "in the juvenile system, where punishment is minimal, if any—let's say there is any." They made an explicit promise that she would face nothing more than "minimal" punishment, even though they never had such an intention. When she finally broke down sobbing and admitted that she had killed her son, she was promptly arrested and charged as an adult with murder. She was held in jail for nearly three years before the charges were dropped, based on a lack of evidence of wrongdoing and a judge's conclusion that her confession had been the product of illegal interrogation. (Unlike most of the other cases to follow, she was one of the lucky ones, at least in the sense that her confession was thrown out of court before she was convicted—although not until after she had spent three years in jail.)

One of the worst forms of deception involves implied promises that statements will not be used against the suspects, or that they will not be prosecuted, because such promises obviously carry the greatest potential for persuading even an innocent person to "to tell the police what they want to hear" if that seems to be the only way to bring a lengthy interrogation to an end. In Massachusetts, one police officer obtained a statement from a suspect after assuring him that the conversation would be "off the record"—and later admitted at his trial that it was a "lie."[40] In Texas, the police got a suspect to talk after falsely promising him that they would be using him "just [as] a witness" in the prosecution of three others who were present at a murder; he was later convicted and sentenced to life in prison.[41] In another Massachusetts case, a suspect agreed to let FBI agents record him making statements that were later used against him, even though those agents had given him promises of "immunity"—but those promises were later broken by the agents and by the Department of Justice. The United States Court of Appeals concluded that was not a problem, because a promise of immunity is no good unless it is authorized by an Assistant United States Attorney.[42] In New York, a confession made after nine hours of interrogation was held to be admissible even if "the police misled him by informing him that he was the least culpable of the suspects and that he would be released if he cooperated."[43] The appellate courts concluded that such promises, even if they were made, were just part of the game that we encourage the police to play. In all these cases, the courts allowed individuals to be convicted in part on the basis of statements they made after the police promised those statements would not be used against them. Is it any wonder that such forms of deception have sometimes been used to deceive even *innocent* people into thinking that they might as well say whatever the police obviously want to hear?

In Mississippi, police officers told a suspect that he might be able to "get it straight" and be out of prison in time to see his four-year-old daughter's first day of school, if he confessed. The court said this offer, because of its seeming specificity, was "more troubling" than those in most similar cases, in which the officer typically makes nothing more than a general promise to bring the suspect's cooperation to the attention of the judge. But the federal trial judge, and later the court of appeals, overlooked that deception because they felt the defendant should have known from prior experience with the criminal justice system that the police cannot be trusted, and that "there were limits on the authority of detectives to bring lesser charges or offer a shortened sentence."[44] But that did not stop those officers from lying to the suspect and using his trust to their advantage: after he agreed to talk, he was convicted and sentenced to over eighty years in federal prison! It would have been much more honest if the officers had told him that he might get out in time to walk his great-granddaughter to her first day of school.

In a California case, a sixteen-year-old defendant agreed to talk to the police only after one of them told him, "The fact is this, Freddy, is I can't *help* you unless you talk to me." He then gave a statement that was used to help convict him, and he was sentenced to life in prison without any possibility of parole. Of course his lawyer argued that he had been deceived and tricked into making this statement, but the California appeals court disagreed, stating that the officer had "offered no leniency in exchange for a confession."[45] That reasoning by the court was no less deceptive than the lie told by the police. Of course the officer was offering leniency in exchange for a confession; what else would possibly be inferred from a police officer telling a young suspect that he wants to "help" that frightened young man? That is exactly what the officer meant to imply, and exactly how he knew his offer of help would be interpreted by the suspect. It is scandalous that the California court would pretend it could not see such an obvious truth.

In Texas, a police officer deceived a murder suspect into giving up his right to remain silent with a similar series of lies. After asking the young man about his age, he told the suspect that he had his "whole life ahead of him," as if to imply that the suspect had the potential to put this matter somehow behind him, even though the officer later admitted he knew that the defendant was going to be charged with capital murder and might be sentenced to death.[46] In the same interrogation, when discussing the fact that the young man had been using crack, the police officer lied by indicating that an unplanned shooting might not even be a criminal offense when he told the suspect: "You know what[,] if this just happened when you, you know[,] you might [have] been doing something you didn't realize what you were doing, that's fine! There's nothing wrong with that." The clear and intended implication was that there might be no criminal liability for a spontaneous act by someone high on crack, when the officer knew that was an absolute lie. The defendant was convicted and sentenced to life in prison.

In Illinois, a criminal suspect named Calvin Montgomery was tricked into talking to federal agents with a similar deception.[47] After he exhibited some initial reluctance to talk to the agents at all, they deceived him into giving up his rights by making a general offer of some sort of unspecified "help." When Montgomery pleaded with the agent, "Can't you just help me?" the agent replied, "I'm helping you more than you know." After Montgomery agreed to talk and gave information that would be used to help convict him, he was then prosecuted, and the government tried to use that statement against him. When the federal judge asked what the agent meant by that promise of help, the agent later testified that "he *meant* to say that he was helping Montgomery by bringing charges against him. If Montgomery took advantage of the substance abuse treatment and vocational training available to him in prison, he would be able to turn his life around." But he never explained that to the suspect, of course, who obviously had no idea that the agent was actually offering to help by putting him in prison. In the same case, the agent also told the defendant, "Well, if you get time, you're not going to get [ten] years." That promise, as it turned out, was true—in a perverse way—because Montgomery was eventually convicted and sentenced to more than fifteen years in prison! But that fact did not trouble the federal courts either.

As we can see from all these cases, a promise from the police to give you "help" is the most useless and worthless promise you will ever receive from anyone in your life, and the courts will laugh and look the other way when the police walk away from that promise without giving you the slightest help in any way. In perhaps the most extreme case of all, one man facing charges of capital murder agreed to talk to the police, after they told him that it "would be better for him" to cooperate with the authorities. He took their word for it, gave them some information that was later used to prosecute and convict him, and he was sentenced to death![48] It is difficult for any open-minded observer to see what kind of "help" he received in exchange for his cooperation with the police. If the police "help you out" by helping you get the death penalty, you might fairly wonder: What is the worse alternative if I don't agree to talk?

***

One of the most egregious cases you could possibly imagine was the outrageous deception used by the police against a seventeen-year-old suspect named Salvador Rubio.[49] He was interrogated by the police in a murder case in which he faced a mandatory minimum prison sentence of forty-five years; in fact, he was ultimately convicted of first-degree murder and sentenced to sixty years. His lawyers argued on appeal that he had been tricked into making statements that were used to help convict him, because the police told him that the sentencing judge would "hammer" a suspect who falsely denied his guilt. They also told him that he still had the chance to "make it right," and that the only reason he should not worry about making it right "is if [he] went out there planning on doing this, planning on killing that guy," as if a lack of premeditation might excuse everything. The officer went on to give Rubio false and worthless legal advice: "If you went out there and this was something that happened spur of the moment, you didn't expect this guy to come out, things got heated, whatever happened[,] happened, and this is the way it ended up, this is the time to make it right. It's not later when you don't have the chance; okay?" Again, the unambiguous and intentional implication was that Rubio could possibly escape serious criminal liability if he got caught up in an unexpected encounter without premeditation, on the spur of the moment. That was a lie, and the police knew it.

But they were not done yet; the officer also told Rubio: "I don't think . . . you're a murderer, man. People who murder people sit out there and plan stuff out and they make their moves and they do everything just perfectly and the whole thing, that's not what this was, this was a sporadic action that happened because a friend was in trouble. I can understand helping a friend out and I can understand that a person gets scared and does something he shouldn't do but for God sakes, . . . don't make this look to be anything more than it is; okay." Just in case Rubio still didn't get the point, the cop added: "But what I'm saying is you're a young man, you got a long life ahead of you and this is something that you can get over; okay? But as long as you're uncooperative, it's not going to look good. If you're remorseful and you're honest about it, that's the part that looks good, that's what I'm saying, you got a good chance of getting by. . . . Put this thing behind you, get it done with, get it over with, explain to us in your own words what happened. The sooner you get this over with the sooner you get on with your life. This is not the end of your life. This is the end of a bad part of your life."

Let's be honest. There is no room for any reasonable disagreement. These statements by the officer were, beyond a shadow of a doubt, plainly intended to convey to Rubio that he could possibly escape serious criminal liability if he cooperated and confessed that he shot someone without premeditation in an unplanned and impulsive act, and could then "make it right" and "get on with his life." But after he was convicted and sentenced to sixty years in prison, the Illinois appellate court concluded that the police had not engaged in any improper deception, and they had not broken any implied promises that they made to Salvador Rubio. In the opinion of the Illinois appellate court, "the detectives did, as defendant notes, consistently contrast [his] alleged actions with more serious crimes, and they did offer that his actions were understandable. However, their comments were limited to *moral* rationalizations for defendant's alleged acts—*they made no comment on the legal implications* of the shooting." (Emphasis mine.) In other words, according to the Illinois courts, it should have been obvious to this young man that the police were not giving him any legal advice (as he might have naturally expected from a police officer), but were simply engaging with him, as he should have realized, in a little bit of banter involving moral philosophy. What pure nonsense.

I do not know whether Salvador Rubio was guilty or innocent, but it is absolutely disgraceful that our nation allowed a seventeen-year-old teenager to be sentenced for sixty years on the basis of tortured judicial logic and evidence that was extracted from a defendant in exchange for promises such as these. Every time I read one of these stories, I cannot help but wonder: How would these judges feel if one of their own teenage children had been tricked into surrendering sixty years of his life? You know the answer, and so do I. They would be outraged. But they don't get too upset when it happens to somebody else's child.

It is possible, although the matter seems debatable, that we could justify all these outrageous forms of deception by the police if there were some way to be sure that all of the people who waive the right to remain silent are guilty. After all, the cynical observer might be tempted to reply, "If we know that they have confessed, that means they are guilty, and so this is just good police work." But that is far too simplistic, for two reasons. First, not everybody who makes an outright confession is in fact guilty, as I have demonstrated, and some of them will later be proved innocent. Besides, not everyone who is tricked into waiving the right to remain silent is in fact making a "confession" of guilt; many of the suspects in the cases I have described here denied their guilt but simply made a partial admission of some fact that was used to help convict them.

The use of dishonesty and trickery by the police always poses a risk of serious injustice, even if it does not cause an innocent person to confess altogether, and even if it only gets him or her to talk just a little bit. As we will see, there are many different ways that the mere act of talking to the police can get you in a great deal of trouble, even if you do not technically admit your guilt, and it almost does not even matter what you say.

The bottom line is clear. Even if you are innocent, the police will do whatever it takes to get you to talk if they think that you might be guilty. That includes saying just about anything, no matter how dishonest, to help persuade you that it might be in your best interest to give them a statement. And the courts will generally say whatever they need to say to excuse the dishonesty on the part of the police, even if the courts have to say something that is just as dishonest. This ought to be a national scandal and not swept under the rug the way that it is. This is not a legal system that is deserving of our respect, much less our cooperation. If a used car salesman engaged in this sort of deception, he would be thrown behind bars. It boggles the mind that we regularly allow police officers to do the same sort of thing to our children—but of course we're only allowing it because we don't know that it is going on.

***

What if you give information to a police officer or any other individual that you think might support your claim of innocence? Will that person be allowed to share that information with the judge or the jury at your trial? The answer will surprise you: no, almost certainly not—not unless it hurts your case. Once the case gets to trial, as you know from television, the police and other witnesses are not allowed to share all the information in their possession—not even if they wanted to do so—because they are subject to a collection of rules known as the *law of evidence*. Those rules define certain kinds of information that are inadmissible, and which therefore cannot be revealed to the judge or the jurors who are deciding the case. And one of the most famous of those rules is the law of hearsay, which generally prevents the police from telling the judge about information that they have heard from other witnesses—including of course the defendant. So even if your lawyer asks the police officer to tell the jury the "helpful things" you told the police to support your claim of innocence, the prosecutor will object, and the judge will usually refuse to allow the officer to answer the question.

But it gets even worse than that. Unfortunately for the defendant, there is a major exception to the hearsay rule in every state and federal court, which does in fact allow the police officer to tell the jury about a statement made by the defendant, or about any portion of his statement, but only if that information is used against the defendant at the request of a *prosecutor* who is trying to prove the defendant's guilt. If a prosecutor asks the officer to tell the jury about portions of the defendant's statement that can be used to help persuade the jury of the accused's guilt, the defendant's lawyer cannot object that this is hearsay, and the testimony will be allowed. But nothing you tell the police will be of any value to *your* lawyer at the trial. That is just one more reason why the police know they are lying when they tell you or your frightened child, "I just want to help you."

We are all familiar with the famous Miranda warnings, written by the Supreme Court a long time ago, which require arresting officers to advise the suspect that, among other things, "anything you say can be used against you in a court of law." The problem with that warning, as most criminal suspects unfortunately do not understand, is that it is literally true. What you tell the police, with extremely rare exceptions, will never be revealed to the jury at your trial *unless* it is offered by the prosecutor and is used to help get you convicted.

Because of these rules of evidence, a prosecutor is allowed to handpick the parts of your statement to the police that might be used against you, reveal those parts to the jury, and keep back the rest. Take for instance Jasper Perdue, who agreed to give a statement to a special agent of the FBI in a bank robbery prosecution.[50] When the case went to trial, the agent testified that the defendant had admitted that he was involved in a robbery, but only as a lookout. The defense attorney was concerned that the agent was only relating a small portion of the conversation and was giving the jury the misleading impression that the defendant had confessed—when in fact, he argued, the overall tenor of the interview had been just the opposite. On cross-examination, he tried to ask the officer several questions in an effort to set before the jury the rest of the story and the rest of the interview, and to confirm that Perdue had not admitted that he had shot the clerk during the robbery. The prosecutor objected, and both the trial judge and the court of appeals held that the officer would not be allowed to answer any questions about the portions of the interview that might have *helped* the defendant. Perdue was convicted and sentenced to prison for 122 years. The United States Court of Appeals said it had no problem with that arrangement, because that is what happens at trials all the time.[51] I have no idea whether Perdue is innocent or guilty, but I can guarantee you this: the FBI agents who told him that it might help his situation if he agreed to talk were lying to him, and they knew it.

In other words, talking to the police is at best a no-win situation for someone suspected of committing a crime. If you talk to the police for three hours and give them three hundred details that would all tend to support your defense, and you only mention three details that might help get you convicted, the prosecutor has every right under the law to ask the officers to only tell the jury about the three details that seem to implicate you in the crime. Do you think the police officers who falsely promised you that they were somehow offering to "help you" by collecting information to present to the judge will regret their lie after you have been convicted? No chance. They have done it to countless other criminal suspects, and they will do it again. But you can be sure that they have already made sure that no police officers will ever do it to one of *their* children.

***

When confronted with police officers and other government agents who suddenly arrive with a bunch of questions, most innocent people mistakenly think to themselves, *Why not talk?*

I haven't done anything. I have nothing to hide. What could possibly go wrong?

Well, among other things, you could end up confessing to a crime you didn't commit—or your child might, if you have not warned them. The problem of false confessions is not some sort of urban legend. It is a documented fact, and extensive psychological research has confirmed how these false confessions can be linked to certain commonly used police interrogation techniques.[52] Indeed, research suggests that the innocent are, ironically, sometimes the most likely to be unfairly influenced by deceptive police interrogation tactics, because they tragically assume that somehow "truth and justice will prevail" later even if they falsely admit their guilt.[53] Nobody knows for sure how often innocent people make false confessions, but as Circuit Judge Alex Kozinski recently observed, "Innocent interrogation subjects confess with surprising frequency."[54]

It happens especially in cases when the suspect is young and vulnerable. A thorough analysis of 125 proven false confessions found that 33 percent of the suspects were juveniles at the time of arrest, and at least 43 percent were either mentally disabled or ill.[55] In Oakland, California, police isolated and interrogated a sixteen-year-old named Felix in the middle of the night without a lawyer and denied his requests to see his mother. Eventually he gave them a *detailed* videotaped confession to a murder, allegedly filled with numerous specifics only the real killer would have known. At that point, it looked like there was little chance this young man would have been able to avoid a conviction; when a jury hears that someone has confessed, they are almost certain to convict. But fortunately for him, it was later revealed that young Felix had an airtight alibi, because he had been locked up in a juvenile detention facility the day of the killing! The charges were then dismissed, and he was released from jail.[56]

Leonard Fraser, fifty-one years old at the time, was charged with murdering Natasha Ryan, then fourteen years old, who had been missing for nearly five years at the time of his murder trial. The prosecution's case was based almost entirely on his recorded confession to the crime, because there was no other substantial evidence of his guilt, but that was enough to persuade the prosecution to go ahead with the case. Late in the trial, however, Fraser received an incredibly lucky break when it was suddenly discovered that Ryan—the woman he'd confessed to having murdered—was discovered alive and well! She had been living in her boyfriend's house for years. The charge was dismissed and the case was thrown out of court.[57] Had Ryan not been discovered during the trial, Fraser almost certainly would have been convicted after he confessed to murdering a woman who wasn't even dead.

Eddie Lowery was a twenty-two-year-old soldier stationed at Fort Riley, Kansas, when he was interrogated for an entire workday about a rape and murder he never committed. Like a typical innocent man, he persisted for hours in emphatic assertions of innocence. Like typical police officers, the interrogators acted open minded and unconvinced. Perhaps, he foolishly hoped, he might persuade them of his innocence if he repeated his story over and over again at greater and greater length. After the day-long interrogation, he was worn out and gave them a *detailed* confession. He served more than twenty years in prison until he was recently released, after evidence proved that he was actually innocent. So why in the world did he confess to such a terrible crime, when we now know that he was innocent all along? He explained the mindset of someone who has been broken down by seven hours of relentless interrogation: "I didn't know any way out of that, except to tell them what they wanted to hear, and then get a lawyer to prove my innocence. . . . You've never been in a situation so intense, and you're naive about your rights. You don't know what [someone] will say to get out of that situation."[58]

One analysis of forty-four proven false-confession cases revealed that more than a third of the interrogations lasted six to twelve hours, many lasted between twelve and twenty-four hours, and the average length was more than sixteen hours.[59] The longer you speak to police officers, the more likely it is that you will confess to some crime that you did not commit—isn't that enough of a reason to avoid speaking to them?

These dangers, of course, are greatest among the most psychologically vulnerable, including the youngest suspects. Another study of 340 exonerations found that 13 percent of the adults falsely confessed compared to a whopping 42 percent of the juveniles.[60] It is unconscionable that our system supports such heinous practices—nearly half of exonerated children were put behind bars because of something they said to police without an attorney present. Someday soon, perhaps when you least expect it, a police officer may receive mistaken information from a confused eyewitness or a liar, or circumstantial evidence that helps persuade him that your child might be guilty of a very serious crime. Under the law, the police do not need to obtain your consent, or even to notify you, before they approach your son, for example, and ask if he will agree to answer their questions. They do not even need a warrant for his arrest if they can deceive him into thinking that it might be a good idea for him to accompany them on a trip to headquarters "voluntarily" to try and clear a few things up. If he is innocent of any misconduct or wrongdoing, he will of course emphatically deny it again and again, perhaps for six hours or more. The problem is that guilty people do the same thing, so the police officers have heard it all a million times and will not be moved at all by his passionate denials. But to keep him talking, they will deliberately *pretend* that perhaps they are uncertain or confused about how they wish to proceed, and they will do this even if they have already decided that he will definitely be arrested no matter how the interview ends. After six hours of relentless questioning, he might well break down and confess in exasperation and exhaustion, perhaps because he foolishly believes that it is his only way to get out of that room. All he needs to do is respectfully tell the police that he will not answer any questions and that he would like a lawyer—the same thing that the officers have instructed their own kids to do in that situation.

***

Do you know where you were on Thursday evening at about eight o'clock last week, and who you were with, and what you were doing? Are you absolutely certain beyond any shadow of a doubt? Would you bet your life on it? If there is any possibility—no matter how slim or remote—that you could possibly be mistaken about such a thing, you are the kind of person who should never agree to talk to the police under just about any circumstances for as long as you live. And that includes practically everybody.

God forbid you should ever come to swear under oath that some incriminating thing you told the police—or that they claim you told them—was not what you meant to say. Far too many jurors who have never been in such a difficult situation will find it impossible to believe that innocent people would ever make the mistake of saying the exact opposite of what they meant to say, even though psychologists understand that this is really not unusual at all.[61]

Even if you do not misspeak by saying something that is different from what you meant to say, you can still incriminate yourself if you make an honest mistake and tell the police something that you thought was true but turns out to be false. When you are talking to a police officer who is investigating a murder or rape, there is no such thing as a little mistake. Every mistake is a big deal and can make it easier for the state to convict you.

Consider the tragic case of Ronald Cotton.[62] He spent more than ten years in a North Carolina prison for a pair of rapes that he did not commit, and he would have been there for the rest of his life if he had not been ultimately exonerated by DNA evidence that proved his innocence and established the identity of the guilty man. When he first learned that the police were looking for him, he foolishly did what most innocent people do under those circumstances: he went down to the police station to meet with them, answer their questions, and attempt to clear things up. He did not take the time to kiss his mother and girlfriend goodbye, because he never imagined he wouldn't be alone with them again for more than a decade. When he was told by the officers about the date of the sexual assaults, he helpfully volunteered some details about his whereabouts, what he had been doing that night, and who he was with. He even invited the police to check with those individuals to verify his story.

Unfortunately for Cotton, he had gotten his dates mixed up, and he'd actually told the police about where he was on another night. As a result, when the police checked with his supposed "alibi witnesses," they were not able to confirm Cotton's story but in fact contradicted it. What he thought would be helpful evidence for his defense had now only made things worse, further arousing the suspicions of the police. After they came back to confront Cotton with the seeming holes in his story, he realized that he had made an innocent mistake and tried to set things right by telling the police where he had actually been that night. But it was way too late, and the damage had been done. What he did not know was that the police had already made up their minds that he was guilty, based upon a fairly confident identification they had received from one of the two victims. But police are only human, as I have said, and witnesses are only human too, and none of them knew of the mistakes they had already made. The police concluded that the information Cotton had volunteered was a sign of his guilt.

If you give the police information that turns out to be inaccurate, and the police mistakenly believe that you were lying to them on purpose, that fact can be devastating to your defense in three different ways. First, it can help to convince the police that they have the right suspect, which might make them less likely to spend additional time pursuing other possible leads that could help them identify the actual offender. Second, the prosecutor can present that evidence to the jury, and the judge will tell the jurors that, if they believe that you knew your statement to the police was false when you said it, they are permitted to regard that knowing falsehood as evidence that you are guilty. (And how will the jury ever really know whether you are lying to the police? They are only human, just like cops.) Third, and perhaps worst of all, our legal system places no limits on the ability of the police to share the details of their ongoing investigation with the critical witnesses against you. When a rape victim is told by the police that "the suspect lied to us about where he was that night"—which in Cotton's case was not true, but they did not know that—it becomes much easier for the witness to convince herself that the "liar" is the one who committed the crime and attacked her.[63] Indeed, that is exactly what happened to Ronald Cotton. The two women he allegedly raped were less than completely confident the first time they saw his face in a photo, and one actually picked out another individual as the attacker. But by the time of Cotton's trial, both women testified that they were completely certain he was the one.

Perhaps the greatest risk of all from giving the police inaccurate and false information is the possibility that the government may decide to prosecute you for the separate criminal offense of lying to the government! Yes, you heard that right: even though our legal system permits and encourages the police to lie to you about almost everything while they are talking to you, it is a federal offense—indeed, it is a felony—for you to make a single statement to the police that you know to be false. Under Title 18 of the United States Code, section 1001, you may be sent to prison for up to five years if you made a single statement to a federal agent that turns out to be false, as long as the prosecutor and the jury can both be persuaded that you knew it was inaccurate.[64] Of course, you might know in your heart that it was just an innocent mistake, as it was for Ronald Cotton, but the police and the jury have no way to know an innocent mistake from a guilty one. They might easily be persuaded that you knew it was a lie when you said it. The proof of your intent is of course only circumstantial, but that is always true in these prosecutions; everybody who is caught in a lie will routinely deny it, so don't expect them to be impressed when you deny it as well. And if you are charged with a violation of this statute, it does not matter whether it was only a single statement about a fairly minor matter, or whether it ever deceived the police or actually affected their investigation.

***

As Mark Twain once famously quipped, the difference between the right word and the wrong word is like the difference between lightning and a lightning bug. Even innocent criminal suspects, when they are a little bit nervous, can say things that they did not mean to say—as we have seen—or accidentally provide mistaken information. But that is only half the problem. The other party to the conversation—the police officer—is also human, just like you, and he or she can make mistakes as well. If an officer's recollection of your conversation is not 100 percent accurate, even an innocuous or innocent remark can become devastating evidence against you.

The most obvious possibility is that a police officer might simply be unsure about exactly what you said, or did not hear you correctly. Maybe it was your fault for not speaking clearly enough, or maybe the officer was having a little trouble hearing that day. Even if it was only one word that was misunderstood, perhaps just a simple little pronoun, it can make all the difference in the world. In one Virginia case, a police officer who tricked a suspect into talking to him (he took advantage of the fact that he was dating the young man's mother, and falsely offered to "help" him) later testified that the first thing the suspect said at the beginning of their interview was, "I messed up," which is of course more or less a confession of guilt.[6] Fortunately for the defendant, however, the police officer was honest and self-aware enough that he was forced to admit that what he might have heard the defendant say was, "*This is* messed up," which is of course a protest that the criminal investigation was focused on the wrong man, a protestation of innocence. The difference between two possibly muffled pronouns in that case was quite literally the difference between guilty and not guilty.

An innocuous statement by a person professing her innocence can be terribly incriminating if someone else does not recall it with perfect accuracy. In California, a woman named Shirley Smith was accused of killing her infant grandson while she babysat for his mother. This woman had no criminal record, no possible motive to hurt this child, and there was no dispute that she loved him deeply. But she foolishly agreed to be interviewed about the death by a social worker, who later turned out to be a key witness against Smith at her trial for the murder of the child. According to the social worker, when Smith was told that the official diagnosis for the child's death had been changed from sudden infant death syndrome to shaken baby syndrome, the heartbroken grandmother supposedly replied, "Oh, my God. Did I do it? Did I do it? Oh my God."[66]

Though these questions were not even a statement, much less a confession, the prosecutor successfully used these alleged questions to help persuade the jury to convict Smith of murder, arguing that no innocent woman would even ask such questions out loud when confronted with such accusations. But another witness who was at the same interview (Smith's daughter and the mother of the victim) denied that Smith had said such a thing, and testified under oath that Smith actually said, "No, I didn't." Unfortunately for Smith, there was no way for sure to resolve what she had actually said. Just a few short one-syllable words can spell the difference between guilty and not guilty. Indeed, even if police officers or social workers correctly recall your response word for word, you may unwittingly incriminate yourself if they mistakenly misinterpreted the inflection of your question ("I killed the baby?" can become "I killed the baby").

Should the police actually understand what you say, there is of course always the danger that they will misremember what you said, or that perhaps they will remember a couple of extra words that you did not say. That is how the Commonwealth of Virginia convicted Earl Ruffin, an innocent man who spent more than twenty years of a life sentence in a Virginia prison for a rape he did not commit, until DNA evidence proved that he was innocent.[67] When he heard the police were looking for him, he voluntarily turned himself in to answer a few questions and to perhaps help their investigation. He knew that he had done nothing wrong, thought perhaps he could help clear things up, and did not see how it could go awry. Stop me if you've heard this one.

When the police officer questioning Ruffin asked where he was on the night of the rape, the officer typed in his notes that Ruffin "stated he was with his girlfriend that night. He said he's sure he was with Rosemary."[68] That information turned out to be 100 percent accurate. When the officer went to check out Ruffin's alibi, he learned that Ruffin was indeed playing a game with his girlfriend, Rosemary, as well as two of their other friends, and all three of those individuals independently verified that the four had spent the evening together. So far, so good. His story checked out, just as he knew it would. So how on earth could that evidence possibly be used to help convict an innocent man? Chances are good that you mistakenly think there is no way, but you would be dead wrong.

When he showed up to testify against Ruffin at the trial, the police officer stunned the attorneys for both sides. He brought with him a copy of his typed notes from the interview with Ruffin, which he had typed up during their interview three months earlier. But now he had changed those notes and had added three more words that were handwritten. Now those new and improved notes contained the report that Ruffin had "said he's sure he was with Rosemary *at her house.*" Those last three words had not been in the notes when they were first typed. Incredibly, the officer did not remember those words until after several months had gone by, and after he claims he sat looking at the notes for more than an hour. The officer also testified under oath that he was "[100] percent sure" that Ruffin had spoken those three words, even though they were left out of the original summary of the interview. The problem for poor Ruffin, unfortunately, was that his three alibi witnesses had all told the police that they were playing together *at his house*, which contradicted the officer's new version of his statement and made him look guilty. Were they telling the truth when they gave that information to the officer? Almost certainly yes. After all, we now know that Ruffin was in fact innocent, as the DNA evidence proved twenty years later, so there would have been no reason for any of them to lie to the police about what he was doing that night.

Just because a well-intentioned police officer suddenly remembered *three words* that had not been in the report before, a statement by the defendant that might have been a key bit of evidence in his defense instantly became a key piece of evidence against him. It was used by the prosecutor to help persuade the jury that Ruffin had lied to the police and had in fact contradicted his own alibi witnesses about where they were that night. And only God knows for sure whether the police also told Ruffin's alleged rape victim about this supposed false information he gave to the police, and the extent to which that information helped solidify her mistaken conclusion that he was in fact the attacker. Both of those possibilities are quite likely—more than probable enough to make any sensible observer realize that only a fool risks talking to the police at all.

It bears repetition, by the way, that poor Earl Ruffin only *thought* that his statement to the police could have been a key bit of evidence in his defense. That was a natural mistake, and innocent people in his position make the same mistake every day and every night, but it is simply not true. As I explained above, the hearsay rules don't allow your lawyer to force the police to tell the jury about things you told the police that might have been helpful to your defense. And so, even if the officer had not later changed his recollection of what Ruffin had said, the defense lawyer would not have been able to prove at that trial that the defendant had given the police that exculpatory account of where he had been the night of the crime.

Of course, Ruffin's trial took place more than twenty years ago, and the danger of what happened to him is slightly less severe for most suspects today, because more interviews these days are being recorded with better-quality equipment, which often leaves less room for doubt about exactly what was said or how it was said. But that is not a complete solution to the problem posed by talking to the police. As incredible as it may sound, even now in the twenty-first century, neither state nor federal agents are obligated under all circumstances to record everything you say to them, and unrecorded conversations are still commonplace around the country. Even if they do agree to turn on the recording equipment, machines sometimes malfunction, and parts of the recording may be inaudible—in which case the courts will never hesitate to let the police tell the jury their best (but usually imperfect) recollection of what was said. And even if a good recording is made of the interview, police officers are routinely allowed to testify about additional statements that they remember you having made before the recorder was turned on, or perhaps after it was turned off. In one recent investigation of forty confirmed false-confession cases, the police recorded some portion of the interview in only 58 percent of the cases—and in *not one* of the cases was there a complete recording of the entire interview before the final statement was recorded.[69]

One of the many terrifying aspects of the police officer's testimony in Ruffin's case was the way it powerfully illustrates the dangers of confirmation bias. There is no reason to believe that the police officer who testified against Earl Ruffin was doing anything to knowingly frame or create evidence against an innocent man. I have no doubt that the officer honestly believed that he had arrested and accused a guilty man of an extremely serious charge. After he accurately typed up some notes about the truthful story he was told about what Ruffin was doing the night of the crime, the police officer went out and interviewed the alibi witnesses—when he discovered that they did indeed back up Ruffin's story! At that point, the officer was starting to get troubled by the appearance that his case was starting to fall apart. By his own admission, the officer then sat by himself staring at those notes for more than one full hour before it suddenly came back to him that his notes had left out three words—and those magical words, by an amazing coincidence, suddenly converted this document into a key bit of evidence for the prosecution! You think that was a coincidence? Don't be absurd. But this happens all the time. Because police officers are only human, their memories sometimes deceive them and enable them to "recollect" things that will confirm whatever it was that they originally said when they publicly staked out some controversial position, like making an accusation against someone they arrested. Ask any experienced prosecutors or criminal defense attorneys, and they will all tell you the same thing: after a police officer arrests you, if he later remembers additional details that he initially forgot to write down, those additional details will *always* confirm the original accusation and help the prosecutor. Those "new memories" will never undermine the original charges and help the defense.

There is only one way to completely eliminate the danger that you might be convicted on the basis of an innocent remark that you made, simply because the police did not quite hear it correctly, or because they did not remember it quite right, or because they remembered a few extra words that you actually did not speak. Do I need to remind you what it is? I doubt it.

***

We have seen that you can get into a great deal of legal trouble even if you are innocent and only tell the police the truth—if the police have any confused or mistaken witness or other evidence that can be used to prove that what you said was false. Accounts of this happening are more common than you could ever imagine. Out of hundreds of innocent people in the United States who were wrongfully convicted and later exonerated by DNA evidence, 76 percent were mistakenly identified by an eyewitness.[70] More than any other factor, eyewitness testimony causes the most wrongful convictions, and confident eyewitnesses—even if mistaken or confused—are notoriously difficult to cross-examine.[71] They are often extraordinarily confident and convincing even when they are totally wrong. It happens all the time.

The dubious "expert" witness, just like the mistaken eyewitness, is another distressingly common way in which the police can discover "evidence" to prove that what you told them was false, even if in fact it was true. How often does this happen? There is no way to know for sure, but it is not unusual. In Boston, Massachusetts, in 2013, a state drug lab was closed, and one of its chemists was convicted on multiple counts of tampering with evidence, after it was discovered that the lab was the origin of thousands of false-positive forensic tests showing a presence of illegal drugs.[72] A few months earlier, in Saint Paul, Minnesota, an independent review found major flaws in the procedures followed by a state crime laboratory in its drug analyses and fingerprint examinations.[73] Expert firearms analysts from the FBI testified around the country at trials in which they falsely claimed that they could actually identify whether two gun shells had been taken from the same box, and such testimony resulted in numerous convictions around the nation—until the FBI itself admitted, to its great embarrassment, that there was never any scientific validity to this testimony.[74] In 2015, the Justice Department and the FBI formally admitted that "nearly every examiner in an elite FBI forensic unit gave flawed testimony in almost all trials in which they offered evidence against criminal defendants over more than a two-decade period before 2000," involving over 2,500 criminal convictions.[75] One national news journal correctly concluded that such scandals are now "occurring with mind-numbing frequency."[76] In one recent and thorough examination of 250 cases in which a convicted prisoner was exonerated by DNA evidence, it was revealed that "forensic evidence" was used to help convict an innocent suspect in 74 percent of the cases,[77] and 61 percent of the scientists and analysts called as prosecution witnesses gave testimony or made claims that were demonstrably invalid.[78]

At the time you make the fateful decision to talk to the police, even if you sincerely believe you have done nothing wrong, you have absolutely no way to know whether your truthful information will later be contradicted by some well-intentioned but mistaken eyewitness, or by some corrupt or incompetent so-called expert witness. The police, the prosecutor, and the jury will not know for sure who is telling the truth, but they will look on your denials with great skepticism. After all, since you are the suspect, you will seem to be the only one with a motive to lie. And as we've seen, a jury can be persuaded that you lied about something when in fact you actually told the truth. Fortunately, there is one very simple way to eliminate that possibility altogether. Don't talk to the police.

***

Even if you strike just the right balance between anxious and cool (both nervousness and calmness have been accepted by the courts as signs of guilt)[79] and are completely innocent, and even if the police understand and recall what you said with 100 percent accuracy and have no evidence that anything you said was false, you may find that just speaking the *truth* can help get you convicted!

You don't need to take my word for it. The Supreme Court of the United States made this point years ago, when it correctly stated that: "[O]ne of the Fifth Amendment's basic functions is to protect innocent men who otherwise might be ensnared by ambiguous circumstances. . . . *[T]ruthful responses of an innocent witness*, as well as those of a wrongdoer, may provide the government with incriminating evidence from the speaker's own mouth."[80]

But how does this happen?

Let me give you three examples—three men who were sent to prison for life, or sentenced to death, and who all spent decades behind bars before they were recently proved innocent. All three were convicted on the basis of unfortunate coincidences and ambiguous circumstances that they were not able to explain away. In all three cases, most of the evidence that they were unable to explain was information that nobody would have even known about—and they never would have had to *try* to explain—had they not volunteered to give that information to the police.

Remember Earl Ruffin? I told you about him already. He was convicted of raping a woman in her Virginia home and sentenced to life in prison, where he spent more than twenty years before DNA proved that he was innocent. One of the things that was used to help convict this innocent man was truthful information that he gave to the police. The police asked him if he knew this woman or if he had ever committed sexual assault against her or anyone else. Ruffin told police the truth: he had never met her, and he had never done such a thing. Then the police asked him if he had ever been in the neighborhood where this crime was committed. Ruffin then made one of the greatest mistakes of his life. Because he actually wanted to cooperate as much as he could and help the police solve this terrible crime, as innocent people usually do, he told the police the truth. Yes, he told them, he once had a girlfriend who lived in that same neighborhood not long before.

Why would Earl volunteer the fact that he once had a girlfriend in the same neighborhood? If he had taken only a second to think about it, he would have immediately realized that there was no possibility that this information would help prove his innocence, assist his defense in any way, persuade the police that they had the wrong guy, or help them find the real rapist. So why did he do it? For the same reason that innocent people constantly make the same terrible mistake: because they think they have nothing to hide, and because they honestly wish to be (or at least to seem) as cooperative as they can with the police.

Unfortunately for Ruffin, as is usually the case, the police had cards they were not laying on the table. Although he did not know it at the time, Ruffin had been brought in for questioning as a suspect not because he had ever been seen in that neighborhood, as far as the police were aware, but because the victim had seen him in the building where she *worked*, miles from where she lived. (Unfortunately, this kind of mistaken identification is not unusual; when a victim has been through a terrible trauma like sexual assault, the natural and overwhelming desire is to spend every waking moment scanning the faces of people nearby, hoping against all odds that perhaps the perpetrator will show up again somewhere. And the danger that the victim will make a mistake is especially great in a case like this one, where the victim was a white woman and the defendant a black man, because all of us have greater difficulty in making reliable cross-racial identifications.)[81]

This means that Ruffin was, unfortunately, the victim of a most unlikely coincidence. Now that the police were aware that he once had a girlfriend in that same neighborhood, they became more certain of his guilt, and that fact was used to help convict him at trial. When Ruffin took the witness stand in his own defense and truthfully testified that he was innocent, almost the entire cross-examination by the prosecutor was devoted to forcing him to admit that he had once spent time in that same neighborhood making regular visits to another woman—a fact that he never would have had to explain to anyone if he had not told the police about it. The prosecutor asked a long line of sarcastic questions, conveying his disbelief in the defendant's insistence that this rape victim had mistakenly picked out a totally innocent man who just happened to have a former girlfriend who lived miles from his home, but in the same neighborhood where that victim was attacked in her home.[82] You have to admit, that does sound a little far-fetched. But it was the truth. Unfortunately for Earl, the prosecutor, just like the police, found that this alleged coincidence was a little too implausible to believe, and apparently the jury did too. But they were all wrong about him, and he spent twenty years locked up in a box because of their mistake. And all because of information—truthful information—that an innocent man foolishly volunteered to give to the police.

Of course, it is certainly possible that Ruffin might have been convicted without that information. After all, there is the possibility that he would have been convicted based only on the testimony by the victim, who said that she was sure he was the one. But we can never know for sure. Truthful information he gave to police might have made the difference between his freedom and two decades in prison.

***

A few years ago, Michael Morton was released from a Texas prison where he had spent almost twenty-five years of a life sentence for a crime that he did not commit.[83] He was released after it was discovered that a corrupt prosecutor had failed to turn over evidence to Morton's lawyers that would have been extremely helpful to the defense, including DNA evidence that practically proved his innocence. The prosecution had virtually no evidence against Morton at all, except for truthful information that he shared voluntarily with the police.

The last time Morton ever saw his wife alive, she was sleeping in their bed when he left for work. Several hours later, while she was home alone with their young son, someone broke into the house and brutally murdered her. There was also evidence that she had been sexually assaulted. But there was never any eyewitness or physical evidence to suggest that Morton had committed the crime. In fact, their son—who saw the murder—later told the police that the killer was *not* his father, but a man he called "a monster." The police and the prosecutor never gave that information to Morton or his lawyers.

When Morton heard about the crime, of course, he was devastated. He instinctively, foolishly, made the terrible decision to talk to the police and tell them the answer to everything they asked him about. By the time they were done with their investigation, they had no direct evidence connecting him to the crime, no witness or physical evidence to prove his guilt. In fact, they had nothing against him at all, except for unfortunate coincidences and ambiguous circumstances that he had willingly shared.

For example, Morton admitted to the police that the night before the murder, he and his wife had been in a little argument.[84] It had been his birthday, and he was disappointed that she had fallen asleep before they could engage in some romantic intimacy. In fact, he had actually left her a handwritten note in their bathroom before he left for work the next morning, expressing his disappointment with that fact. In the opinion of the prosecutor, and then the jury, and then the Texas Supreme Court, this evidence was the most important evidence against Morton, because it showed his supposed motive to commit the crime. There were many other details that Morton gave the police—truthful answers from an innocent man—that were also used to help convict him. For example, when the police asked where and when Morton had eaten dinner with his wife the night before, he made a terrible mistake of telling the police the truth. (Why do I say that it was a terrible mistake? Because, just like the information Earl Ruffin gave the police about his former girlfriend, it was information that could not possibly help his defense, or help the police identify the true killer.) He revealed to the police that he and his wife had eaten dinner together at a local restaurant at about nine thirty in the evening.

Before I go any further, I need to ask you to take a moment and consider the following question: How on earth could evidence like that possibly be used to help convict an innocent person? If an innocent man like Morton tells the police where and when he had taken his wife out to dinner the night of his birthday, how could that be used to help implicate him in her murder at their home the next day? Even if you are unusually intelligent and imaginative, chances are that you will have to admit to yourself, *I cannot possibly see how that could be used against him.* But you would be wrong.

When Morton told the police the time that he had dinner with his wife, he was unwittingly giving the government what turned out to be "critical evidence" against him, because any evidence that you give to the police, even truthful information, can be used to help convict you if it is interpreted by an incompetent or corrupt expert witness. And there are countless bogus experts out there, all more than willing to testify in exchange for the generous compensation that is paid to them by willing prosecutors who are anxious to make a case against the only suspect they can find.

In Michael Morton's case, the prosecutor called a witness at trial who offered his "expert opinion" that, based upon his examination of the contents of Morton's wife's stomach following her autopsy, she was killed within four hours of her last meal. This testimony was simply wrong, as we now know, because we all now know that Morton was innocent, and that his wife was not killed until after he'd left for work. But this junk science supposedly *proved* that Morton was alone with his wife at the time of her killing, because he was the one who told the police what time they had dinner together, and because he was the one who told the police what time he left for work! The police never would have been able to make that argument if Morton had not spoken to them.

***

Just two years ago, Glenn Ford was released from a Louisiana prison, where he had spent more than twenty-nine years on death row, awaiting execution for a murder that he did not commit. He was released after the local prosecutor revealed that they had evidence in their possession to prove that he could not have committed the crime.[85] To make matters even worse, Ford learned shortly after his release that he had lung cancer, and he died a few months later at the age of sixty-five. There is absolutely no way that he would have been convicted of anything had he exercised his right to remain silent. The police had no evidence against him except for the truthful information that they were given by this innocent man.

About thirty years ago, in the New Orleans area, a jewelry merchant was found shot and killed in his store.[86] There were no witnesses, no fingerprints, no photos or videos of the killer or the killing. The police had almost nothing to go on. When they interviewed the victim's friends and neighbors, no surprise, they found that the victim had a number of acquaintances with whom he was in occasional contact. One of those individuals was Glenn Ford, a black handyman whom the dealer sometimes employed to fix things around the store. The police naturally decided that they would question Ford to see what he might know.

Ford should have sent word to the police in writing, perhaps through an attorney, that he knew about their interest in meeting with him, but that he would very respectfully decline to answer any of their questions. But that is not what Ford did. And if you have been reading this book from the beginning, by now you can of course guess his tragic mistake. Just like most innocent men who foolishly think they have nothing to hide, Ford went down to police headquarters in the middle of the night to talk with them. He did not take a lawyer, although he did go with his father. Surely neither man ever imagined that they would never again see each other alive outside of a jail cell.

Ford did not admit that he was guilty, because he was not. He told the police truthfully that he did not commit the crime, that he was not there at the time of the shooting, and that he had no idea who had committed the crime. (Even that was a mistake. Even if that was all he had told the police, it could have possibly been used to help convict him, as we have seen, if the officer had any mistaken eyewitnesses or experts who would claim that he was there at the time, or if the police thought he seemed suspiciously nervous or calm.) But he did not stop there. He also told police that, by an unfortunate coincidence, he had been at the jewelry shop, apparently just a few hours before the shooting, and had asked the merchant if he had any work for Ford to do. When the merchant said he had no work to offer, Ford asked if he could borrow some money in advance. But the merchant declined that request as well. Ford told the police that he then left the store. There was no other witness to that meeting, and no way the police could have learned those details from any other source if Ford had not told them himself. But armed with this information, the police and the prosecutor concluded that Ford had both the motive and the opportunity to commit the crime.

To make matters worse, Ford also admitted that, right after he left the jewelry store, he walked around to the back and urinated in the alley behind the store. Why did he tell the police such a thing? It certainly could not have helped him look more innocent, or help the police find the real killer. But this is what innocent people do when they talk to the police—they keep talking for hours, volunteering everything they can possibly think of, even if it could not possibly help anyone except a corrupt prosecutor. That detail certainly did not prove that he was guilty, but it was mentioned by the prosecutor at the trial, and even mentioned later by the Louisiana Supreme Court when it summarized the relevant "evidence" against Ford. Apparently they interpreted his act as if it somehow confirmed his malice or hostility.

When the police asked if Ford had any alibi witnesses who could verify where he was at the time of the killing, he was very happy to tell them that he did have such witnesses, and he volunteered their names and contact information. But when the police met with those alibi witnesses, they turned out to be worse than useless for Ford's defense. They tried to be helpful, because they told the police that Ford was indeed with them at what the police and their expert thought was apparently the time of the killing. Can you guess what happened next? That's right: after the police found that Ford had alibi witnesses who could verify that he was with them at the apparent time of the killing (which is not unusual for an innocent suspect), their "expert" changed his opinion about the likely time of the death. Now the killing was placed at a time when Ford's witnesses could not verify his whereabouts; suddenly those witnesses became useless to Ford. But they were not useless to the prosecutor.

The police also learned from these alibi witnesses that not long after the killing, Ford had discussed with them his desire to sell a gun in his possession. There was no evidence that Ford owned or used the gun illegally, or that he desired to sell the handgun in a manner that would violate the law. But in the opinion of the police and the prosecutor and the jury and the state supreme court, this was just too much to write off as mere "coincidence." Under Louisiana law, Ford could not be convicted on the basis of such circumstantial evidence unless it was enough to exclude beyond all reasonable doubt any alternative hypothesis that was consistent with his innocence. But the jury and the state supreme court both concluded there was no way that all of these incriminating and suspicious details could possibly be written off as innocent coincidence. Ford was then sentenced to death, and it took more than thirty years for everybody to learn that he was entirely innocent—and convicted on the basis of *nothing* but information and leads that he had volunteered when he met with the police that night.

***

Any time you agree to talk to the police or government investigators, you are rolling the dice and taking a terrible chance with your life. You do not know what you are up against, because you do not necessarily know what crime they are really investigating. They may tell you, but what they say may be a lie. You also do not know what evidence they already think they have against you. They may tell you, but again, they might only be lying. And even if you are completely innocent, there is absolutely no way you could possibly have any idea whether the truthful details you give the police could tragically get you ensnared in a web of ambiguous circumstances, later leaving you in the position of trying in vain to convince the jury that it was all just an amazing coincidence.

I once heard a young prosecutor telling a jury in closing argument that "there are no coincidences," and he seemed perfectly sincere. The obvious problem is that there really *are* coincidences—that is why we have a word for them—and some of them are so extraordinarily implausible that they almost defy belief. A few years ago, a young couple in South Africa met in college, fell in love, and became engaged before they discovered that they were biological siblings, raised by their estranged parents in separate cities.[87] Two lovers in England were married before they learned that they were actually *twins* who had been adopted by separate families as babies.[88] Two California girls met in an online hunt for roommates after they chose to attend the same college in Louisiana, then became close friends and later roommates before they discovered that they were born in different cities to different mothers but had the same biological father.[89] Such things are so strange and bizarre that they are hard to believe, but in a world with more than seven billion people, just about anything can happen once in a while.

Unfortunately for innocent criminal suspects, their life and liberty rest in the hands of prosecutors, jurors, and even appellate judges who have no specialized training or insight into probability or statistics. Heaven help the poor fool who volunteers the remarkable fact that he once had a girlfriend in the same neighborhood where some victim mistakenly says he raped her, or the fact that he had an argument over sex with his wife the night before somebody else broke into their house and killed and sexually assaulted her, or the fact that he was trying to sell a gun not long after somebody *else* shot a man who refused to give that suspect some money that same day. At that point, your only hope is to pray that your lawyer can help persuade the jury that these suspicious circumstances were just a "coincidence." You may know in your heart that you were telling the truth and are totally innocent, but you may still spend the rest of your life sitting in a prison cell pondering how unlikely it all was.

***

Let me show you just how easily the police can trick you, either deliberately or unintentionally, into making an incriminating statement. Take a look at the following short report about what the police found recently at a crime scene. Read it over once to yourself, just once, but read it nice and slowly, out loud if you prefer:

> Earlier today at 8:00 a.m. in Miami, Florida, special agents of the Miami Police Department revealed that they had found the bodies of two nursing students who had been sexually assaulted and murdered in their apartment. The two victims were roommates at the Miami University Department of Nursing. Their bodies were found

and identified for the police by Diana Wilson, a young woman who was the twin sister of one of the victims. Police estimate that the victims were killed sometime around midnight, although their bodies were not found until shortly after sunrise.

Now that you have read that short story, see if you can answer the following questions correctly *without* looking back at the facts you have just read about this crime report.

1. In what city and state did the crime take place?
2. How many women were found murdered at that crime scene?
3. What sort of a college were they attending?
4. What time do police think the crime took place?

After you have read and answered those four questions, ask yourself: Are you *certain* about the accuracy of some or all of your answers? Absolutely certain? So sure that you would be willing to risk your life and liberty? Remember your answers to those questions for just a couple minutes, but do not go back yet to see if you are right or wrong. The truth will astound you.

In the last few years, as I have traveled around the country speaking about the Fifth Amendment, I have asked my audiences these same questions after reading them the same fictional news report about a crime scene in Miami. Every time

I do, I ask the audience members to listen as closely as they can as I read them this narrative. I warn them in advance that I will be questioning them on what they have heard, so they are listening very closely. In fact, in order to give them the greatest possible motivation to listen as closely as they have ever listened to anything in their lives, I even warn them that I will be trying to trick them.

The set of facts I give them, as you saw for yourself, is short and sweet and takes less than thirty seconds to read slowly. And I might add that these audiences are far above average in terms of their linguistic sophistication, as they are law students, lawyers, or judges, all well rested and seated comfortably at a daytime conference—nothing like a typical individual, perhaps just a teenager, who is being questioned for hours in the middle of the night by people who think this person has done something terrible that he or she did not do. And yet, of the many hundreds of individuals who have taken this little quiz at my request, nearly 100 percent get it wrong, as you almost certainly did as well.

Of course, they get most of the questions right, as I am sure you did, but when I ask how many women were found killed at the crime scene, virtually everybody raises their hand high in the air, confident and without any hesitation, in order to assure me that they distinctly remember me saying that two women were found at the scene. (You remember that as well, don't you?) I put this question to nearly a thousand audience members in the last three years, and only two or three have shown any hesitation in insisting that they heard me say such a thing.

Go back and read it again. I never said that two women were found at the crime scene. I said nothing about their sex or gender at all. I said that there were two *victims*, but I was very careful not to tip my hand or to say whether they were two men, or two women, or one of each. You thought I said that, but you were wrong. Go back and look again, and you will see for yourself. And yet look how *certain* you were just a minute ago about what you were sure that you had read. Why did you make that mistake? Perhaps it was because I told you that they were nursing students, or because they were victims of sexual assault, and you probably knew that a high percentage of both of those groups are women. But not all of them. Or maybe you were misled when you read that one of the victims had a twin sister. Most people who have a twin sister are women. But not all of them; some men have twin sisters. Of course, in your defense, it is true that you were making a reasonable assumption, and it is true that a very large percentage of nursing students with twin sisters are women. But that is not the point.

The point I am trying to demonstrate is how often and easily you and I make assumptions and deductions, drawing conclusions and inferences from what we have been told, without even being aware of the fact that we are doing it. And that is why it is so extremely easy for police officers, just like everyone else, to mislead you into doing the same thing even when they have no awareness that they are doing it either. And look how easily you were deceived in just thirty seconds, even though you were able to read this statement with your own eyes, and even though I warned you in advance that I would do this to you. Now just imagine how much easier it would be for the police to do the same thing to you, either intentionally or otherwise, when they are selectively feeding you details about a crime for several hours in the middle of the night.

What I have just demonstrated—that your memory can deceive you—can cause unimaginable grief in a criminal investigation. Suppose you have been questioned by the police, perhaps for several minutes, or maybe several hours. They have given you a great deal of information about the crime, although not all of it is accurate, and some of it is intentionally false. You have met with several officers during the interrogation, some of whom may have been in the room at different times, in addition to another officer who had escorted you downtown, and another one who had brought you a cup of coffee. Some of them have been feeding you different details about the case, while others merely mentioned them in your presence. At one point in the questioning, possibly after hours of this informal process, one of them tells you that the victim has identified you as the attacker. In exhaustion and frustration, you turn to the police and respond, "Then she is either lying or mistaken, because I never attacked anyone." Then you shut up and ask for a lawyer (just a few seconds too late, as it turns out) and refuse to say anything else.

Could that simple little one-sentence denial somehow be used to convict you of a crime that you did not commit? Absolutely yes, without a doubt, and it happens all the time. But how? How could the police officer and the prosecutor use against you the fact that you made a simple denial of your guilt? Here's how it has played out, again and again, in case after case around the country. When the case against you finally goes to trial, here is what the jury will hear from the prosecutor and the police officer:

Q. Officer Krupke, did the defendant say anything to you at all?

A. Almost nothing, but what he did say was extremely significant

Q. Oh? What was it?

A. When I told him that the victim had identified him as the attacker, the defendant became indignant, and suddenly replied—here, let me read to you from my notes—"Then she is either lying or mistaken, because I never attacked anyone."

Q. I am confused, officer. Why was that statement so significant?

A. Because we never told him that the victim was a woman. He was the first one to make any mention of the gender of the victim!

You see what they did there, don't you? At this point, the jury will gasp and wheel around to face the defendant, who will return their gaze with a nervous and confused look, even if he is totally innocent. But the poor jurors will naturally think that they have just heard the "case cracker." The officer will then proceed to explain how he was trained at the academy to very carefully and skillfully refrain from disclosing too many details to the suspect, and how he followed those instructions in this case, all so that he could possibly trip the suspect into revealing that he knew (wait for it) details that "only the real criminal would have known."

This happens all the time, probably every day of the week. In one New York case, a police officer testified that, when the defendant was brought to the station for a lineup behind a one-way mirror, he asked one of the officers afterward, "Did she really pick me out?" That simple little question is not incriminating at all by itself, but it became extremely damning evidence of guilt after the officer insisted that he had never told the defendant that the victim was a woman, or had even mentioned it in his presence.[90] The defendant in that position then has to explain, if he can, how and when he thinks he overheard some police officer mention that detail, but now it is his word against the police's. And guess who will win that argument almost every time?

This trick works so well in obtaining incriminating statements from guilty suspects, some police officers simply cannot stop there, and they routinely use it against innocent suspects as well. One recent study of proven false confessions from innocent suspects revealed that almost *every one* of them (thirty-eight out of forty confessions) was full of extremely incriminating details that "only the real killer would have known"—which all sounded extremely damning, until you find out that all of these confessions have come from someone who is totally innocent.[91] (I told you about one of those cases earlier, involving a sixteen-year-old named Felix who allegedly gave such a confession to the police before they found out that he was locked up in a juvenile detention center on the day of the crime!)

How does this happen? How could it possibly be the case that a perfectly innocent man could give a confession, or even just a short statement, or maybe just ask the police a single *question*, that seems to prove that he knew some details about the crime, even though the police will invariably swear that they never told him about those details? Perhaps the officer simply does not know, or cannot correctly remember, every word of exactly what was said in the suspect's presence while he was at the station house for several hours. Or maybe the suspect simply assumed that he was told some detail that he actually was not told—just as I tricked you moments ago into thinking that I told you about two *women* when I said no such thing.

In ordinary conversations, all of us are constantly making assumptions and deductions based upon things that our interlocutors did not actually say, but which we gather that they meant to imply. It saves us all a great deal of time, and it is all just harmless fun in the context of a chat between two friends. But this natural human tendency, which normally works in ways we do not even perceive, can get you into a great deal of difficulty if you ever agree to talk to the police. Even if you were not present at the scene of a crime and know nothing about it, it is impossible for you to answer questions (or just to make truthful denials) about that event for several hours without eventually slipping up and unintentionally revealing that you have made an assumption about something that you were not actually told. And heaven help you if even one of those assumptions turns out to be true, because then you have just incriminated yourself.

***

Every American over the age of five knows a little bit about the Fifth Amendment to the United States Constitution, and the right of every citizen to not be a witness against himself. Most Americans are not aware, however, of just how unspeakably precious this right is for every criminal suspect, even the innocent. That is why, tragically, the vast majority of all people who believe they have nothing to hide willingly agree to waive their Fifth Amendment privilege and talk with the police. But you now understand why that mistake is a foolish and tragic gambit. And now you also understand why police officers and prosecutors around the country advise their own children not to talk to the police, while at the same time they give the opposite advice to everybody else's children.

At this point, many readers might be tempted to put this book down, thinking to themselves, *OK, I get the picture, and now I understand what I need to do. If the police ever ask me whether I want to talk with them, I will simply remain silent. Or else maybe I will tell them I want to assert my right to remain silent.* But it is not that simple at all. Either one of those choices, believe it or not, could prove a different kind of mistake, one no less grave and imperiling as talking in the first place.

II

DON'T PLEAD THE FIFTH

If I ask my son whether he saw a movie I had forbidden him to watch, and he remains silent, the import of his silence is clear.

> —Supreme Court Justice Antonin Scalia, *Mitchell v. United States*, 526 U.S. 314, 332 (1999) (dissenting opinion)

Until a few years ago, most judges and lawyers believed that one's silence in the face of questioning by the police could not be used as evidence of one's guilt. In fact, not long ago, the Supreme Court wrote that "evidence of silence at the time of arrest" generally does not tell us very much about guilt or innocence. The court correctly recognized that "at the time of arrest and during custodial interrogation, innocent and guilty alike—perhaps particularly the innocent—may find the situation so intimidating that they may choose to stand mute."[1] That is why the Supreme Court also stated that the Fifth Amendment privilege, "while sometimes a shelter to the guilty, is *often* a protection to the innocent."[2] As a result, the Supreme Court back then held that a prosecutor was not allowed to tell the jury about the fact that a defendant had invoked his right to remain silent.[3]

In other words, the Supreme Court understood that the Fifth Amendment was written for the protection of both the innocent and the guilty, and that *both* groups have many reasons for asserting the privilege. In the last several decades, however, a conservative majority has emerged on the Supreme

Court and undermined the basic protection of your right to remain silent.

Few men or women in our lifetimes have been so unjustly vilified in the popular media as the late Justice Antonin Scalia of the United States Supreme Court. If you are not a lawyer who read his opinions, if you know nothing about Justice Scalia other than what you have read in the popular press, you have surely been deceived into believing that this man was some sort of archconservative who could regularly be counted upon to side with the government and trample the constitutional liberties of the poor and the powerless. The truth is much more complicated than that. While Justice Scalia was, by his own admission, exceptionally stingy in refusing to accept arguments about constitutional rights that involved some aspect of general "liberty" that are not explicitly mentioned in the Constitution—rights like abortion, or same-sex marriage—when it came to the defense of constitutional liberties that are *explicitly* described in the Constitution, no other recent member of the Supreme Court was so uncompromisingly passionate and liberal in refusing to water down those protections.[4]

But with all due respect to Justice Scalia for his passionate defense of the most precious constitutional rights that are explicitly laid out in the Bill of Rights, nobody else on the court has been such an articulate and ardent proponent of the view that the Fifth Amendment privilege only protects the guilty, and that innocent people have no reason to even assert, much less treasure, that privilege. And Justice Scalia used that misguided assumption, as well as his considerable influence on the court, to help shape the development of American constitutional doctrine in ways that have endangered anyone pulled into a criminal investigation.

The conservative majority on the Supreme Court, under the eloquent leadership of Justice Scalia, accepted three of the most monstrous and dangerous lies that have ever been sold to the court by the prosecutors of the nation:

1. They believe that only guilty people would ever knowingly refuse to talk to the police, because the innocent have nothing to hide. Justice Scalia talked a majority of his colleagues into joining an opinion that he wrote, in which he sincerely but mistakenly asserted that the problems caused by the risk of self-incrimination are "wholly of the guilty suspect's own making," because "[a]n innocent person will not find himself in a similar quandary."[5]

2. And since the court now believes that the innocent have nothing to fear from the police, the Supreme Court has mistakenly reasoned that nothing but good can come out of a legal system that gives the police every possible tool and incentive to get you to waive your right to remain silent. The Supreme Court has recently held several times, again in a line of opinions written by Justice Scalia, that it is not evil but "an unmitigated good" when criminal suspects voluntarily agree to make a

statement that can be used to help convict them.[6] That is pain-fully false, and it would be true only if nobody but a guilty man could possibly get himself convicted by talking to the police.

3. And because of that mistaken assumption, a conservative majority of the court now agrees that when a criminal suspect does decide to remain silent, that fact logically supports the conclusion that the suspect must be guilty. Justice Scalia has put the point this way: "If I ask my son whether he saw a movie I had forbidden him to watch, and he remains silent, the import of his silence is clear."[7] Justice Scalia's assessment of his son's silence makes perfect sense, but his analogy was nonsense. With all due respect, he simply did not understand the reasons why young men interrogated by their fathers do not face the same perils encountered by innocent suspects who are questioned by a police officer they do not know, as this book has explained. His mistaken intuition is also plainly refuted by a study of innocent prisoners who were convicted of crimes they didn't commit only to be cleared by DNA evidence, which found that 39 percent of those innocent defendants had decided *not* to testify at the trial where they were falsely convicted.[8] It is absolutely false to suggest that the silence of the accused is important evidence of guilt.

Because of this mistake, the Supreme Court made legal history when it held just three years ago that the silence of a criminal suspect in the presence of the police does in fact support the conclusion that he or she must have something to hide.[9] In the case of *Salinas v. Texas*, decided in 2013, the five most conservative justices on the court (the only five appointed by Republican presidents) held for the first time that the silence of a criminal suspect, at least if the suspect is not in custody, is logically relevant evidence that is admissible against the suspect at trial and may be used to help persuade the jury that the suspect is guilty! Those five members of the court agreed that the State of Texas was therefore within its rights to prove and argue that a young man named Genovevo Salinas was probably guilty of a crime because he remained silent when the police asked him a question about it.

Incredibly, the Supreme Court was also persuaded to adopt this position by the supposedly liberal administration of President Barack Obama and the Department of Justice led by Attorney General Eric Holder (who, Obama later said, has "worked passionately to make sure our criminal justice system remains the best in the world").[10]

Shortly before his recent death, Justice Scalia candidly confessed that "we federal judges live in a world apart from the vast majority of Americans,"[11] which is so heartbreakingly true. Justice Sonia Sotomayor, lamenting the lack of diversity on the Supreme Court, recently complained that "there is no criminal defense lawyer on the court."[12] Even Justice Kagan, one of the supposed liberals on the court, confessed that one of the best things about her new job is that she no longer has to go through security at airports.[13] Small wonder, therefore, that these justices are in over their heads when called upon to imagine what perils are posed by police encounters for the rest of us ordinary Americans.

The *Salinas* decision was tragic for so many different reasons, including the fact that the court was simply wrong about the pivotal assumption that only guilty people have any reason to remain silent. But it was unbearably ironic that the court would reach that result in a case like this one, because the precise question that young Genovevo "suspiciously" refused to answer from a police officer was whether shells from a shotgun that Genovevo owned "would match the shells recovered at the scene of the murder." Even if he was completely innocent and knew nothing about this alleged murder, his refusal to answer a question like *that one* was exceptionally smart, for all the reasons outlined in this book. There is no way that I would have answered it, and I have practiced and taught criminal law for more than thirty years. But if I had been in Genovevo's position and knew I was totally innocent, and if I only had a few days to live and nothing to lose, I would have been tempted to say this much to the officer:

Seriously? You want me to guess whether you are going to be able to find a so-called expert who will testify that my gun matches the shotgun shells you claim you found at the scene of some murder I know nothing about? Are you out of your mind? I gather that you have not yet seen the *60 Minutes* special "Evidence of Injustice," which exposes how a number of men around the country have been convicted on the basis of expert testimony from FBI agents who *falsely* claimed that they could match shotgun shells as coming from the same box, even though it later turned out that there was no scientific basis for that bogus testimony. Even though I know nothing about this crime you are talking about, and I know that my gun had nothing to do with it, I also know that if I tell you that you will not find a match between those shotgun shells, you might well find some cockamamy expert who will mistakenly conclude that there *was* a match. At that point, even if you do not have any significant evidence that I committed this supposed murder—and for all I know, you might be lying to me about whether there was a murder, and may only be investigating some sort of shooting—I can then be charged and prosecuted for my alleged offense of lying to you about whether that gun was fired at the scene! So no, Officer, with all due respect, I will not put my liberty on the line and run the risk of becoming the next false conviction by trying to guess what your so-called expert witness will conclude about those shotgun shells.

But there was one small ray of hope for innocent American citizens in the *Salinas* decision. In ruling against Genovevo Salinas, the Supreme Court noted that there were two reasons why his silence was admissible against him as evidence of his guilt. First, he was not under arrest or in custody at the time he remained silent—and the Supreme Court long ago held that your silence cannot be used as evidence against you if you refuse to answer questions after you are under arrest.[14] Second, when he was asked about those shotgun shells, he did not affirmatively assert his right to remain silent, but instead simply remained mute. The conservatives on the Supreme Court thought that was not enough to protect his rights, but stated (without deciding) that he *might* have won the case if instead he had spoken up and told the police that he did not want to incriminate himself.

In the aftermath of the *Salinas* case, therefore, criminal suspects now have—for the first time in American history—a new reason why they must *not* simply remain mute when they are questioned by the police. If you simply say nothing in the face of police questions, unless you are in custody and under arrest, your silence can and will be used against you as evidence of your supposed guilt in a court of law. To avoid that possibility, you must speak up and specifically tell the police about your desire to assert your constitutional rights.

But exactly what do you say, and how do you say it?

The Supreme Court did not decide the answer to that question in the *Salinas* case. So I will tell you. I doubt that anyone who has read this far in the book will have any difficulty understanding the importance of your constitutional Fifth Amendment privilege to remain silent, and of not answering questions that might be used to help incriminate you. But we need to briefly consider a few surprising rules about *how* you should exercise your right to remain silent.

There are a couple rules you must observe about what you should say, and what you must not say. And as you will see, most of them are so unnatural and counterintuitive that you probably would not have guessed *any* of them on your own. Fortunately, they are not too difficult to memorize and pass on to others. Let me list them for you, and explain why they are so important.

You Must Explicitly Invoke Your Constitutional Rights

In any encounter with the police, you have several different objectives to keep in mind. Of course, as we have seen, your primary objective is to make sure that you do not say anything that could be used against you, which means that you will say virtually nothing at all. But the problem is that you cannot remain absolutely mute, because you have two other important objectives that you must also accomplish at the same time, and neither of those will be completed if you remain completely silent.

First, you need to make sure that your silence is not held against you as evidence of your guilt if the case later goes to trial. And after *Salinas*, as we have seen, that means that you cannot simply remain mute in the face of police questioning, but rather must say something to invoke your legal right to refuse to answer their questions.

Second, you also need to make sure that you get the police to stop questioning you and leave you alone. You need to bring the interrogation to an end, once and for all, and as quickly as possible. But that will not happen unless you say something. Just a few years ago, the Supreme Court held that a man who sat almost entirely silent for nearly *three hours* in the face of continuous police questioning had not in fact made a valid assertion or exercise of his right to remain silent.[15] According to the Supreme Court, his extended silence was merely ambiguous as to whether perhaps he wanted to talk to the police. The conservatives on the court apparently thought that when a person looks at you without saying a single word while you sit there asking questions for three hours, it is possible that person is still trying to make up his or her mind about whether to speak or not! (It would be fascinating to watch those justices at breakfast with their spouses.) Consequently, the court held, the police were entitled to continue to question that man until they finally wore down his resolve, broke his will, and got him to talk. All because he did not make an effective assertion of his rights.

You Must Not Tell a Lie

Years ago, First Lady Nancy Reagan, the wife of President Ronald Reagan, launched a nationwide antidrug campaign with the slogan "Just say no." That was great advice for young people talking to drug dealers. But it was terrible advice for young people who talk to the police.

As we learned earlier in this book, even innocent people must be exceptionally cautious when dealing with the police, making sure they do not say anything that might later subject them to the separate charge of lying to the police. When a police officer comes to ask you about a crime that you did not commit, ironically, you may find yourself getting into legal trouble if you say anything—or if the officer recalls that you said something—that sounds like a *denial* of something the officer thinks can be proven. Because that means you have just committed a crime that can get you sent to prison for up to five years.

This means that you must speak with a great deal of precision when you are explaining yourself to the police, which is easier said than done. If you are an ordinary American who is not accustomed to expressing yourself in such a clear way, you may easily be tempted to make the terrible mistake of thinking that perhaps you can "just say no" when questioned about something you would rather not discuss. That natural mistake has gotten some people in a great deal of trouble. One criminal suspect was charged with lying to the police when he told them, "I don't know what you are talking about." The government later charged and proved that he was lying when he said that, because they were able to convince a jury that he *did* have some information about what they were asking him about.[16] Obviously there is a very fine line between telling the police, "I do not wish to discuss this matter," and, "I do not know anything about this matter." Indeed, they are so close that a careless police officer might not recall clearly which one was an accurate quotation of what you said—but the former is the exercise of a constitutional privilege, and the latter may be a federal criminal offense.

Just a few months ago, Susan Thompson, a fifty-eight-year-old widow with no criminal record, worked for the federal government at the US Army Corps of Engineers.[17] She was approached by a federal agent, who asked whether she had placed a picture of a Confederate flag on the desk of an African American coworker. The agent was not from the FBI—they have infinitely more important things to worry about—but was instead an agent of (I am not making this up) the United States Federal Protective Service. You have probably never even heard of this organization, which is the security police division of the National Protection and Programs Directorate, a division of the United States Department of Homeland Security. I swear that I think I saw some of those organizations mentioned somewhere in George Orwell's *1984*. According to the agent, when he asked Ms. Thompson whether she had done such a thing, she said she had not.

If this woman actually left a picture of a Confederate flag on the coworker's desk, of course, that was rude and offensive, and many would agree that it was downright despicable. But it was probably not a criminal offense, much less a felony. (But just like any other lawyer in the country, I could *not* confidently assure her that such conduct could not be prosecuted under any of the thousands of federal criminal statutes on the books, which is why any lawyer would have advised her to not answer that question.) Indeed, it is even possible that her action might have been a form of free speech protected by the First Amendment to the Constitution.

But it is now entirely academic whether she might have committed a crime when she placed that flag on someone else's desk, because the Obama Department of Justice has instead charged this woman in federal court with two counts of the separate offense of lying to federal agents when she denied putting it there. If she had been convicted of both charges, she faced the possibility of as much as ten years in prison—simply because she denied committing a certain act, which might not have even been a crime, and which might have even been protected by the First Amendment.[18] Who in their right mind would ever imagine that you could actually go to prison for lying about whether you did something that might not even be a crime? That is why Supreme Court Justice Ruth Bader Ginsburg sensibly complained years ago about this very same statute and voiced her grave concern over what she called "the extraordinary authority Congress, perhaps unwittingly, has conferred on prosecutors to manufacture crimes."[19]

The astonishing fact illustrated by this story, which would probably come as a tremendous surprise to almost everyone who is not a lawyer, is the breathtaking ease with which any federal agency—when it has too much time on its hands—can turn almost anyone into a criminal, simply by way of a few unexpected and nonthreatening questions about something stupid or embarrassing (not necessarily criminal) that they already know or suspect you have done. They can then take advantage of the terribly unfortunate but 100-percent-understandable tendency on the part of almost every fool in that situation to immediately think:

> *I cannot admit that I did such a stupid thing, and it will look suspicious if I refuse to answer, so maybe I better lie about it and say that I did not do it. I know I should not lie to anyone, because that is wrong, and I promise myself I will never do it again after today, but surely it cannot be a crime to tell a little innocent lie to stay out of trouble. Why, I have been telling little lies to keep myself out of trouble all my life, especially when I am dealing with government agents; I do it almost every time I am pulled over by the police when they ask me how fast I was driving. And since the Fifth Amendment gives me the constitutional right to refuse to answer his questions at all, surely it cannot make a big difference whether I refuse to answer his question and say nothing, or take Nancy Reagan's advice and just say* no.

That poor soul will later learn that he was absolutely wrong and may have made the biggest mistake of his life.

To make matters worse, the possibility of such insane criminal prosecutions is readily increasing as our federal government is growing rapidly out of control. Here is just a partial list of some of the more than forty United States federal agencies that now employ a total of 120,000 armed investigative agents: the National Park Service, the IRS, the Postal Inspection Service, the Department of Health and Human Services, the Departments of Agriculture, Labor, and Veterans Affairs, the Environmental Protection Agency, the Fish and Wildlife Service, the Bureaus of Land Management and Indian Affairs, the Small Business Administration, the Railroad Retirement Board, and the Federal Reserve Board. Even the Library of Congress.[20] ("You mind if we come in to ask you a few questions about an overdue book?")

When one of *these* people comes by your office to meet with you, you must always and absolutely refuse to speak with the agent—even if you are dating this person's son or daughter—because they are the most dangerous people in our country. Unlike agents from the FBI, who have their hands full trying to enforce the most important criminal laws and catch the most dangerous criminals, most of these government agents wage a daily effort just to justify their existence, and to explain (at least to themselves) why they should even have a job, not to mention a gun and a badge and a pile of blank search warrants. Avoid them like the plague.

If you want some recent examples, just google the madness caused for the Gibson guitar company by agents of the Fish and Wildlife Service, who cost the company half a million dollars because of their investigation of some wood that may have been imported in violation of some Indian laws designed to protect local jobs in India.[21] Or read about the insanity that was inflicted on Nancy Black, a dedicated and respected marine biologist, who spent her life savings and years of her life defending herself against charges that she lied to agents of the National Oceanic and Atmospheric Administration, an agency of the United States Department of Commerce.[22] I *know* that you have not already read about those two investigations, because you would not have needed to read this book if you had heard about either one of those real-life horror stories of governmental bureaucracy utterly out of control.

More than a year ago, one of my clients was approached by a federal agent who was investigating some possible criminal activity, and who asked if she would be willing to answer a few questions on a voluntary basis. The agent, who worked for a certain federal agency that I will not name, dropped by my client's house a couple times, always without warning. My client asked for my advice. I told her to send the agent a letter, explaining that she would be happy to consider answering any questions he might have, but only if he would extend her the minimal courtesy of putting those questions in writing, so that she could also put her answers in writing. What on earth would be so unreasonable about a request like that? Nothing at all. It would enable this woman to think carefully about her answers, possibly obtain the assistance of a lawyer, and check her records to make sure that her answers were accurate. It would also eliminate the very terrible danger, discussed at great length in this book, that the agent might later unintentionally misquote her in ways that could make her statements sound more damaging than they really were. The request was perfectly reasonable—and, I might add, it was exactly what any federal agency will tell you to do if you want to get important information out of them. ("Put it in writing, and we will get back to you in a couple months. Maybe.")

But that was the end of the investigation, as I knew it would be. When the federal agent was advised that my client would not talk to him unless he was willing to put his questions in writing, he angrily replied that he refused to interview anybody that way, and she has not heard from him in months. Just think about that. That tells you just about everything you need to know about the motives of this government agent. He was more than happy to talk to my client as long as he could have the element of surprise and the ability to hold all the cards by asking her a bunch of questions in an informal interview that would not be recorded—and he knew from years of experience that he would have no difficulty getting any jury or judge to believe him if he later testified from his notes about his recollection of that conversation. But when he was asked if he would simply agree to allow the exchange to be put in writing, he refused. That is the kind of unreasonable behavior you can expect when a government agent has become spoiled through years of always having it his way, dealing only with people who are never able to effectively contradict his recollection of exactly what was said, and by whom.

Don't Plead the Fifth

The Department of Justice a couple years ago helped to persuade the Supreme Court that prosecutors should be allowed to tell juries about the fact that a suspect who was not in custody tried to exercise the right to remain silent if the suspect did not tell the police explicitly why. So that means you should tell the police that you wish to exercise your privilege against self-incrimination, right? Wrong. The same year the Supreme Court decided *Salinas*, the Department of Justice also helped persuade another federal court in another case that it should be lawful and permissible for a prosecutor to argue that anyone who explicitly asserts the right against self-incrimination is *also* admitting guilt.

In early 2008, Gillman Long was living on an Indian reservation in South Dakota. He was approached by a special agent from the FBI, Sherry Rice, who said he was not under arrest, but she wanted to talk to him about some allegations.[23] The agent persuaded Long to meet with her at a nearby tribal office on a voluntary basis. She told him again that he was not under arrest and could end the interview at any time. She then told him about some allegations about him by a minor—his girlfriend's niece—concerning improper sexual contact. Long replied by describing an incident in which he said he was sitting at a computer in his house when the alleged victim came up and rubbed her breasts against his back; he insisted that he then stood up and pushed her away. At that point in the interview, according to the FBI agent, Long allegedly said, "I do not want to incriminate myself. I would like to stop talking."

At the end of the trial in federal court, once the case had gone before a jury, the Assistant United States Attorney began her rebuttal closing argument not by discussing the testimony of the alleged victim, but instead by asking the jurors to focus on the defendant's assertion of his constitutional rights. She began her closing argument with these words:

> "I don't want to incriminate myself." That was what Gillman Long said to Agent Sherry Rice when she asked him about sexual contact between him and [the alleged victim]. . . . What was his response? "I don't want to incriminate myself."

Then, after advising the jurors that they could "never use [it] against somebody when [that person] invoke[s] the right to remain silent," the prosecutor said in complete contradiction, "We are asking you not to leave your common sense at the door. If somebody doesn't want to incriminate themselves, it means any sort of statement as to that topic that they are being asked for would get them in trouble."

Of course, the prosecutor's argument was absolutely false. As this book has clearly demonstrated, and as even the Supreme Court understood fifty years ago, innocent people have ample reason to fear the perils of talking to the police, and they therefore have a perfectly lawful right to refuse to give answers to questions that might incriminate them. But partly on the basis of this argument, Long was found guilty and sentenced to life in prison without any possibility of parole. On appeal, the Obama Department of Justice successfully persuaded the United States Court of Appeals that this argument was proper, or at least not clearly improper, and therefore should not result in a new trial. Unfortunately for Long, his attorney had not objected when the prosecutor made those arguments, and the judge who was herself a former federal prosecutor—did not immediately intervene to emphatically contradict the prosecutor, as a good judge would have done. The court of appeals did not decide whether Long might have won if his lawyer had made the right objection, but agreed with the prosecution that the law was ambiguous enough to permit the government to regard this sort of argument as a proper basis for urging a jury to convict a man and take away his liberty for the rest of his life.

The Department of Justice has now served official notice that it believes the courts should allow a prosecutor to argue under any circumstances that your willingness to assert the Fifth Amendment privilege can and should be used against you as evidence of your guilt. It is too soon to know whether all of the federal courts will yet go along with that radical suggestion, but at least one circuit of the United States Court of Appeals has already done so, and the grave danger is that others will follow suit.

What does this mean for the liberty of ordinary American citizens? The implication is as obvious as it is shocking. In light of the ongoing war now being waged against the Fifth Amendment by the federal courts and the Department of Justice, the precious constitutional privilege against self-incrimination is no less important than in the past, but it has now become "the constitutional privilege that dare not speak its name."

III

PLEAD THE SIXTH

*Anybody who understands what goes on during a
police interrogation asks for a lawyer and shuts up.*[1]

—Professor Franklin E. Zimring,
UC Berkeley School of Law, 2015

I f you are asked any question by a police officer or a government agent and you realize that it is not in your best interest to answer, you should not mention the Fifth Amendment privilege or tell the police that you wish to exercise your right to avoid incriminating yourself. In this day and age, there is too great a danger that the police and the prosecutor might later persuade the judge to use that statement against you as evidence of your guilt. And if they do, to make matters much worse, you have no guarantee that the FBI agent in your case will not slightly misremember your exact words. Even if you take care to say, "I wish to invoke my right under the Fifth Amendment against self-incrimination," you have no guarantee that the agent will not testify months later at your trial that "he said he would not talk because the truth would incriminate him." Even if the officer only gets a few words wrong, it only takes a slight rewording of the privilege to make it sound like a confession.

So what do you do instead?

Instead mention your Sixth Amendment right to a lawyer, and tell the police that you want a lawyer. Is that honest? Not entirely, because it sounds like you are implying that you might be willing to talk to them after a lawyer shows up, and of course that is not true, and your lawyer will not agree to that. But a little dishonesty is a small price to pay to defend your freedom and your constitutional rights, especially when dealing with police officers who will lie to you until the sun goes down. And most of them will not stop when the sun goes down if they are being paid by the hour and can get overtime for lying to you through the night.

By invoking your Sixth Amendment right, if you are charged with a crime and the prosecutor wants to use your invocation of that right against you, you will probably be able to keep that information away from the jury under the law, because the federal courts (at least so far) generally agree that you cannot tell the jury that the defendant has asserted the Sixth Amendment right to a lawyer, or to use that as evidence against the defendant.[2] And even if you cannot keep it out of the evidence at trial and the jury is allowed to learn what you said to the agent, it will sound *far* less suspicious if you merely told the officer that you wanted a lawyer present before you agreed to be interviewed. That makes it sound, after all, like you were willing to answer their questions. (But don't worry about what will happen after the police obtain a lawyer to represent you, because they probably will not even bother wasting their time. They know that the lawyer will tell you not to answer their questions.)

But how do you request a lawyer? There is no need to be rude, naturally. And most people instinctively recognize that fact. The police officer does not deserve your disrespect, because he or she is only doing his or her job in a criminal justice system that is terribly out of control.

Unfortunately, far too many individuals in the real world go in the opposite direction, and for some reason think that they need to be overly *polite* to the police. They seem to instinctively fear that they might come across sounding a little rude or disrespectful if they make their request sound too confident or unequivocal. So here are some of the things that actual criminal suspects have said in real cases, when they were trying in vain to end the interrogation and keep themselves out of trouble:

- "Maybe I should talk to a lawyer."
- "[B]ut, excuse me, if I am right, I can have a lawyer present through all this, right?"
- "I think I would like to talk to a lawyer."
- "What time will I see a lawyer?"
- "I think I want a lawyer."
- "I can't afford a lawyer but is there anyway [sic] I can get one?"
- "Could I call my lawyer?"
- "I think I need a lawyer."
- "Do you think I need a lawyer?"

Every single one of the above quotations was taken directly from the mouth of a criminal suspect who was trying to ask for a lawyer, but who tragically decided that he might sound more polite and respectful if he did not act too confident about his desire.[3] In every one of these cases, the police ignored the suspect's tentative and mealymouthed expressions of interest in a lawyer, persisted in their questioning, and successfully managed to get him to make some damaging statements (not necessarily a confession) that could be used to help convict him, and the courts concluded that such statements were admissible against the suspect because he had not made a clear and unequivocal request for a lawyer. In dealing with the police, that kind of politeness is a tragic mistake. In many of these cases, the suspect never would have been convicted if he had simply made his request unambiguous—and we will never know for sure how many of them were indeed innocent, although I have already shown you how easily and how often innocent people can be convicted on the basis of "incriminating" statements they made—or allegedly made.

Even when you try to express yourself rather directly and forcefully when talking to the police, you may become the tragic victim of the ambiguity in your unarticulated punctuation! Tio Sessoms was only nineteen years old when he learned that he was being sought for questioning by California police officers in connection with a murder.[4] On the advice of his father, he turned himself in to the authorities, and he was later questioned by the police after spending four days in custody. At the very beginning of the interview, even before he was told about his right to remain silent, Sessoms tried to prevent them from questioning him. But in an unfortunate desire to sound as polite as he possibly could, he expressed himself this way: "There wouldn't be any possible way that I could have a . . . a lawyer present while we do this?" Obviously that would not be enough to do the trick. But then he went on—and here I am typing it just as he said it on the recorded statement, without adding any punctuation—and added: "Yeah that's what my dad asked me to ask you guys uh give me a lawyer."

You see the problem, of course. Although Sessoms knew that his statement was being recorded by the police, he did not actually dictate the punctuation that he had in mind, so the recorded statement was ambiguous as to which of the following he meant to say:

1. "That's what my dad asked me to ask you guys. Give me a lawyer."

2. "That's what my dad asked me to ask you guys: give me a lawyer."

If Sessoms had simply told the police, without hesitation or equivocation, "Give me a lawyer," that would have been the end of the interview. The same would have been true if he had paused long enough between the two sentences to make clear that they were indeed two different sentences, and that he was in fact *following* his father's advice. Or if he had put it in writing. But he did not do any of those things, and the way he actually expressed himself left itself open to the possibility that he was merely trying to *summarize* his father's advice. It was not clear, the police later insisted, whether this request for a lawyer was just something his father had recommended, or one that he was making himself.

Because of this tragic ambiguity in what we might call the "intended punctuation" of his comments, the California courts ruled that Tio Sessoms had not made an effective request for an attorney, and so his later statements could be used against him at trial. He was convicted of murder and sentenced to life in prison without the possibility of parole. Some good news recently came for Sessoms when his lawyers finally succeeded, after more than ten years of fighting on appeal, to persuade the United States Court of Appeals that he had indeed made a valid expression of his desire for a lawyer, and so his statement should not have been used against him, and that he is therefore entitled to a new trial. But the bad news, as I said, is that it took his lawyers more than a decade of fighting on appeal to win him that result, and by that time he had already been in prison for more than thirteen years. And all because his attempt to invoke his right to counsel, despite its seeming clarity, precision, and forcefulness, was plagued by a bit of arguable ambiguity with respect to how he meant for it to be *punctuated*. The difference between a period and a colon could have cost him thirteen years in prison, perhaps for a crime he did not commit.

There is only one way to avoid this problem. When you ask for a lawyer, do not worry about sounding polite, because that will make you sound unduly tentative or equivocal. Never ask the police officers what their opinion might be. In fact, do not ask *any* questions when you insist on the presence of a lawyer. Do not even use the words *I think* or *might* or *maybe*. You need to say, with no adverbs, in only four words, "I want a lawyer." And then you need to say it again, and again, until the police finally give up and realize they are dealing with someone who knows how our legal system really works.

ENDNOTES

PART I

1   Paul Blumenthal, "Lois Lerner, IRS Scandal Figure, Will Invoke Fifth Amendment at Oversight Hearing," *Huffington Post*, last modified May 22, 2013, http://www.huffingtonpost.com/2013/05/21/lois-lerner-irs-scandal_n_3314693.html. For more recent examples of the same phenomenon, see Laura Koran, "Clinton IT Staffer Intends to Take the Fifth in Upcoming Deposition," *CNN News*, June 2, 2016, http://www.cnn.com/2016/06/01/politics/bryan-pagliano-hillary-clinton-email-server/; Radley Balko, "The South Carolina Police Files: Gunslinging Raids, Coverups and Magical Dog Sniffs," *The Washington Post*, May 31, 2016 (noting that officers pleaded the Fifth Amendment and refused to testify against the men they arrested after videos "revealed major discrepancies in the police's account of their interactions with both men"), https://www.washingtonpost

.com/news/the-watch/wp/2016/05/31/the-south-carolina
-police-files-gunslinging-raids-coverups-and-magical-dog
-sniffs/.

2   Hiibel v. Sixth Judicial District Court of Nevada, 542 U.S.
     177 (2004).

3   At the risk of stating the obvious, you should of course talk to
     the police (although as briefly as possible) in those situations
     in which the law requires you to call them (to let them know,
     for example, that you have been involved in an automobile
     accident or a shooting in which someone has been seriously
     injured or killed), or if you are a witness to or the victim
     of a crime, or if you are pulled over on the highway for a
     minor traffic infraction. These situations have nothing to do
     with our central focus, which is to tell you how to handle a
     situation in which a police officer or other government agent
     comes to you without warning, in an encounter you neither
     requested nor proposed, and wants to ask you some questions
     about where you have been, who you have been with, and
     what you have done.

4   In one recent criminal case, a Texas police officer admit-
     ted under oath in court that he had knowingly lied to
     deceive a suspect into talking, and "that lying is a common
     and accepted police tactic during interrogation." Weaver v.
     State, 2008 WL 2548807 (Tex. App. June 26, 2008). For a
     description of some of the methods of deception the police
     are trained to use, see Brandon L. Garrett, *Convicting the
     Innocent: Where Criminal Prosecutions Go Wrong* (Cambridge:
     Harvard University Press, 2011), 22–23.

5   Garrett, "Contaminated Confessions," *Convicting the
     Innocent*, 18.

6   This information has been compiled by the Innocence Project, which has managed to obtain exoneration and release of over three hundred innocent men and women. "False Confessions or Admissions," Innocence Project, http://www.innocenceproject.org/causes/false-confessions-admissions/.

7   From 2000 through 2007, Congress created, on average, one new crime a week for every week of every year. Brian W. Walsh and Tiffany M. Joslyn, *Without Intent: How Congress Is Eroding the Criminal Intent Requirement in Federal Law* (Washington, DC: Heritage Foundation, April 2010), 8, http://www.heritage.org/research/reports/2010/05/without-intent.

8   Paul Rosenzweig, "The Over-Criminalization of Social and Economic Conduct," *Champion*, August 2003, 28.

9   "In addition to the thousands of criminal offenses spread throughout the [forty-nine] titles of the United States Code, according to estimates tens of thousands of criminal offenses are similarly scattered throughout the over [two hundred] volumes of federal regulations." Walsh and Joslyn, *Without Intent*, 25.

10   Rubin v. United States, 525 U.S. 990 (1998) (Breyer, J., dissenting from denial of certiorari).

11   Edwin Meese III, introduction to *One Nation Under Arrest: How Crazy Laws, Rogue Prosecutors, and Activist Judges Threaten Your Liberty*, ed. Paul Rosenzweig and Brian W. Walsh (Washington, DC: The Heritage Foundation, 2010), xv.

12   *Id.* at xii.

13   18 U.S.C. sec. 707.

14   18 U.S.C. sec. 711a.

15   18 U.S.C. sec. 46.

16   18 U.S.C. sec. 708.

17   Associated Press, "Kennedys' Sea Turtle Rescue Violated Federal Law, Officials Say," *Fox News*, July 17, 2013, http://www.foxnews.com/politics/2013/07/17/kennedys-sea-turtle-rescue-violated-federal-law-official-say.html.

18   For more examples of this madness, see the daily parade of examples on the Twitter feed "A Crime a Day," https://twitter.com/crimeaday. And take a look at the article by Yale law professor Stephen L. Carter, who notes (among other crimes) that it is a federal crime to disturb the mud in a cave on federal land, so he cautions: "Be careful where you run to get out of the rain." Stephen L. Carter, "Over-Legislating Puts Everyone in the Same Danger as Eric Garner," *Syracuse.com*, last modified December 4, 2014, http://www.syracuse.com/opinion/index.ssf/2014/12/over-legislating_puts_everyone_in_the_same_danger_as_eric_garner_commentary.html.

19   16 U.S.C. sec. 3372 (emphasis added).

20   David McNab was one of several individuals prosecuted, convicted, and sentenced to prison for importing lobsters that were smaller than what was allegedly allowed under Honduran administrative regulations. See Rosenzweig and Walsh, *One Nation Under Arrest*, chap. 1.

21   7 U.S.C. sec. 13(a)(2) (emphasis added).

22   18 U.S.C. sec. 229 (emphasis added).

23   Bond v. United States, 134 S. Ct. 2077, 2091 (2014).

24   *Code of Virginia*, sec. 29.1-521.

25   Bill Sizemore, "Freshman Lawmaker Taking His Job by the Horns," *Virginian-Pilot*, February 2, 2010. Luckily for him, however, he was white, and a newly elected member of the "good old boys club," so his violation of the law was forgiven and overlooked. But he was technically guilty and could have been prosecuted under the statute.

26   Harvey Silverglate, *Three Felonies a Day: How the Feds Target the Innocent* (New York: Encounter Books, 2009).

27   Alex Kozinski and Misha Tseytlin, "You're (Probably) a Federal Criminal," in *In The Name of Justice*, ed. Timothy Lynch (Washington, DC: Cato Institute, 2009), 44.

28   For numerous examples, read Rosenzweig and Walsh, *One Nation Under Arrest*. This book is filled with real-life horror stories of people prosecuted, and most of them convicted, for conduct that no man in his right mind would think could even get him in any legal trouble, much less be a crime.

29   The chemicals were 10-chloro-10H-phenoxarsine (an arsenic-based compound) and potassium dichromate (commonly used in printing photographs or cleaning laboratory equipment).

30   *Bond*, 134 S. Ct. 2077, 2091.

31   *Bond*, 134 S. Ct. 2077, 2091.

32   *Bond*, 134 S. Ct. 2077 at 2101 (Scalia, J., concurring).

33 Yates v. United States, 135 S. Ct. 1074 (2015). When Yates's vessel was boarded by a state conservation officer, federal regulations required fishermen to immediately release red grouper less than 20 inches long. The agent testified that he found six dozen fish on board barely below that length, although not one was shorter than 18.75 inches. Yates was indicted and tried in federal court for disposing of the fish before he got to dock, despite the fact that the minimum length for Gulf red grouper had been lowered to 18 inches by the time he was charged!

34 *Id.* at 1101 (Kagan, J., dissenting).

35 *Id.* at 1100–1101 (Kagan, J., dissenting).

36 Moran v. Burbine, 475 U.S. 412 (1986).

37 For numerous examples of such police deception, see Miriam Gohara, "A Lie for a Lie: False Confessions and the Case for Reconsidering the Legality of Deceptive Interrogation Techniques," *Fordham Urban Law Journal* 33 (2006): 791, 801–3.

38 Fox v. Hayes, 600 F.3d 819, 828 (7th Cir. 2010).

39 David Boeri, "How a Teen's Coerced Confession Set Her Free," *All Things Considered*, NPR, December 30, 2011, http://www.npr.org/2012/01/02/144489360/how-a-teens -coerced-confession-set-her-free.

40 Commonwealth v. Tremblay, 460 Mass. 199 (2011).

41 Harris v. State, 2008 WL 2736891 (Texas Ct. App. July 2008).

42   United States v. Flemmi, 225 F.3d 78, 91 (1st Cir. 2000).

43   People v. Alexander, 51 A.D.3d 1380, 857 N.Y.S.2d 418 (N.Y. App. Div. 2008).

44   United States v. Turner, 674 F.3d 420 (5th Cir. 2012).

45   People v. Slordia, 2009 WL 851057 (Cal. App. 2009).

46   Weaver v. State, 2008 WL 2548807 (Tex. App. 2008).

47   United States v. Montgomery, 555 F.3d 623 (7th Cir. 2009).

48   Bolder v. Armontrout, 921 F.2d 1359 (8th Cir. 1990).

49   All of the following facts are taken from the opinion in People v. Rubio, 911 N.E.2d 1216 (Ill. App. 2009). That opinion was reversed by the Illinois Supreme Court, which directed the lower appellate court to consider the case one more time. But after doing so, the court reached the same conclusion and once again affirmed Rubio's conviction and sentence in an unpublished opinion.

50   United States v. Ford, 761 F.3d 641, 651–52 (6th Cir. 2014).

51   For examples of other very recent cases where the courts did the same thing—allowing the prosecutor and his witnesses to tell the jury only about the parts of the defendant's statement that might help result in a conviction, while not allowing the defense lawyers to ask about the *other* parts of the statement in which the suspect tried to deny his guilt or explain his defense—see United States v. Liera-Morales, 759 F.3d 1105 (9th Cir. 2014), and United States v. Dotson, 715 F.3d 576 (6th Cir. 2013).

52   Saul M. Kassin, "On the Psychology of Confessions: Does Innocence Put Innocents at Risk?" *American Psychologist* 60, no. 3 (2005): 215–28.

53   *Id.* at 224.

54   Sessoms v. Grounds, 776 F.3d 615, 631 (9th Cir. 2015) (dissenting opinion). See Saul M. Kassin et al., "Police-Induced Confessions: Risk Factors and Recommendations," *Law and Human Behavior* 34, no. 3 (2009): 3–5; Brandon L. Garrett, "Judging Innocence," *Columbia Law Review* 108, no. 55 (2008): 88–89.

55   Garrett, "Contaminated Confessions," *Convicting the Innocent*, 38.

56   David K. Shipler, "Why Do Innocent People Confess?," Sunday Review, *New York Times*, February 23, 2012.

57   "Alleged Australian Murder Victim Found Alive," *Guardian*, April 11, 2003.

58   John Schwartz, "Confessing to Crime, but Innocent," *New York Times*, September 13, 2010.

59   Danielle E. Chojnacki, Michael D. Cicchini, and Lawrence T. White, "An Empirical Basis for the Admission of Expert Testimony on False Confessions," *Arizona State Law Journal* 40 (Spring 2008): 1, 17–18.

60   Samuel R. Gross, Kristen Jacoby, Daniel J. Matheson, Nicholas Montgomery, and Sujata Patil, "Exonerations in the United States 1989 through 2003," *Journal of Criminal Law and Criminology* 95, no. 2 (2005): 523.

61   The entire world got an unusually dramatic illustration of
      this phenomenon in April 2015 when the city of Baltimore,
      Maryland, erupted in riotous violence after a young man
      named Freddie Gray was killed while in police custody.
      Amid otherwise peaceful protests, a few angry people caused
      massive property damage. The next day, Baltimore Mayor
      Stephanie Rawlings-Blake spoke at a press conference in a
      carefully measured tone of voice, choosing her words
      carefully as she proceeded to say the exact opposite of what
      she meant: "While we tried to make sure that they were
      protected from the cars and the other, you know, things that
      were going on, we also gave those who wished to destroy
      space to do that as well." (See https://www.youtube.com
      /watch?v=9_5KQC7k8Lc.) Yes, the elected Mayor of a
      great American city mistakenly asserted that her office had
      intentionally provided space for people to "destroy" private
      property. The following day she corrected herself: she had
      meant to say that the city had set aside a safe place for people
      who wanted to protest in peace, and the rioters had taken
      advantage of that civic right. But that is not what she said.

62   Jennifer Thompson-Cannino and Ronald Cotton, *Picking
      Cotton: Our Memoir of Injustice and Redemption*, with Erin
      Torneo (New York: St. Martin's Press, 2009).

63   Psychological studies have confirmed that even a mistaken
      witness who is presented with evidence that seemingly
      confirms his or her identification of a suspect will, for that
      reason, naturally become much more confident in that
      identification and therefore a more convincing witness at
      trial. John Gibeaut, "Confidence Boost: Study Shows Police
      Can Convince Eyewitnesses That They Identified the Right
      Suspect," *ABA Journal* 83 (May 1997): 26.

64   Under the federal statute 18 U.S.C. sec. 1001, it is a felony
      to make a false statement concerning "any matter within
      the jurisdiction of any department or agency of the United
      States," but the law is not limited to statements made to fed-
      eral agents. It also applies to allegedly false statements made
      to state and local government agents, as long as they worked
      for a state agency which was involved in the implementation
      of a federal regulation or received federal funding—which
      these days includes just about every state agency—even if you
      did not know about their connection to the federal govern-
      ment. United States v. Wright, 988 F.2d 1036 (10th Cir.
      1993); United States v. Herring, 916 F.2d 1543 (11th Cir.
      1990).

65   Ferguson v. Commonwealth, 52 Va. App. 324, 663 S.E.2d
      505 (Va. App. 2008).

66   Cavazos v. Smith, 132 S. Ct. 2 (2011).

67   Tim McGlone, "Earl Ruffin, the Wrong Man," *Virginian-
      Pilot*, Feb. 8, 2004.

68   All of these details about Ruffin's trial are taken from the offi-
      cial transcript of his trial, a copy of which is in my possession.

69   Garrett, "Contaminated Confessions," *Convicting the
      Innocent*, 32.

70   Garrett, "Eyewitness Misidentifications," *Convicting the
      Innocent*, 48.

71   "The Causes of Wrongful Conviction," Innocence Project,
      accessed May 13, 2016, http://www.innocenceproject.org
      /causes-wrongful-conviction.

72   Mark Hansen, "Crimes in the Lab," *ABA Journal* 99, no. 9
      (September 2013): 46.

73   *Id.* at 46.

74   "Evidence of Injustice," *60 Minutes*, last modified
      September 12, 2008, http://www.cbsnews.com/news
      /evidence-of-injustice/.

75   Spencer S. Hsu, "FBI Admits Flaws in Hair Analysis Over
      Decades," *Washington Post*, April 18, 2015.

76   Hansen, "Crimes in the Lab," 47.

77   Garrett, "Flawed Forensics," *Convicting the Innocent*, 89.

78   Garrett, "Flawed Forensics," *Convicting the Innocent*, 9.

79   A criminal conviction may be based, in part, on police testi-
      mony that the defendant seemed unusually nervous, Morton
      v. State, 283 P.3d 249 (Kan. App. 2012), or unusually calm;
      Avent v. Commonwealth, 279 Va. 175, 688 S.E.2d 244
      (2010).

80   Ohio v. Reiner, 532 U.S. 17, 20 (2001) (emphasis added;
      citations and internal punctuation omitted).

81   Garrett, *Convicting the Innocent*, 12–14.

82   This is a fair paraphrase of the central thrust of the cross-
      examination. I have a copy of the trial transcript in my
      possession.

83   Josh Levs, "Innocent Man: How Inmate Michael Morton
      Lost 25 Years of His Life," *CNN News*, last modified

December 4, 2013, http://www.cnn.com/2013/12/04/justice/exonerated-prisoner-update-michael-morton/.

84 These details about the evidence the police learned from Morton are all taken from the opinion of the Texas Court of Appeals back in 1988, explaining why it was satisfied that he had a fair trial and was fairly convicted based on the evidence against him. Morton v. State of Texas, 761 S.W.2d 876 (Tex. App. 1988).

85 Martha Neil, "Death-Row Inmate Released After 30 Years; Evidence Shows He Was Elsewhere at Time of Murder," *ABA Journal*, March 11, 2014.

86 These details about the evidence the police learned from Ford, and from the leads he gave them, are all taken from the opinion of the Supreme Court of Louisiana back in 1986, explaining why it was satisfied that he had a fair trial and was fairly convicted based on the evidence against him. State of Louisiana v. Ford, 489 S.2d 1250 (La. 1986).

87 Stewart Maclean, "Engaged Couple Discover They Are Brother and Sister When Their Parents Meet Just before Wedding," *Daily Mail*, November 3, 2011, http://www.dailymail.co.uk/news/article-2057081/Engaged-couple-discover-brother-sister-parents-meet-days-wedding.html.

88 "Parted-At-Birth Twins 'Married,'" *BBC News*, last modified January 11, 2008, http://news.bbc.co.uk/2/hi/7182817.stm.

89 Eliott C. McLaughlin, "Sudden Sisters: Tulane Pals Learn They Share Sperm-Donor Dad," *CNN*, last modified January 24, 2014, http://www.cnn.com/2014/01/24/living/tulane-sperm-donor-sisters/.

90   People of the State of New York v. Calabria, 3 N.Y.3d 80, 83
      (2004).

91   Garrett, "Contaminated Confessions," *Convicting the
      Innocent*, 18–19.

PART II

1   United States v. Hale, 422 U.S. 171, 177, 180 (1975) (inter-
      nal punctuation omitted).

2   Carter v. Kentucky, 450 U.S. 288, 299–300 (1981) (empha-
      sis added).

3   Miranda v. Arizona, 384 U.S. 436, 468 n.37 (1966).

4   More than any current or recent justice on the Supreme
      Court of the United States, Justice Antonin Scalia was an
      uncommonly passionate and uncompromising defender of
      the most basic individual liberties that are explicitly enumer-
      ated in the Bill of Rights, including in cases in which those
      rights are asserted by the most unpopular and politically
      powerless members of society. This has been true in contexts
      as diverse as the First Amendment right to free expression
      of unpopular views, Hill v. Colorado, 530 U.S. 703, 741
      (2000) (Scalia, J., dissenting); Texas v. Johnson, 491 U.S. 397
      (1989), the Second Amendment right to bear arms, District
      of Columbia v. Heller, 554 U.S. 570 (2008), the Fourth
      Amendment right to be free of unreasonable warrantless
      searches, United States v. Jones, 132 S. Ct. 945 (2012); Kyllo
      v. United States, 533 U.S. 27 (2001); Arizona v. Hicks, 480
      U.S. 321 (1987), the Sixth Amendment right of the accused
      to a trial by jury in a criminal case, Blakely v. Washington,

542 U.S. 296 (2004), the Sixth Amendment right of the accused to demand that the witnesses against him be brought to the courthouse, Melendez-Diaz v. Massachusetts, 557 U.S. 305 (2009); Giles v. California, 554 U.S. 353 (2008); Crawford v. Washington, 541 U.S. 36 (2004), the Sixth Amendment right to demand face-to-face confrontation with those witnesses who are brought to court, Coy v. Iowa, 487 U.S. 1012 (1988), and the Sixth Amendment right of a criminal defendant to counsel of his own choice, United States v. Gonzalez-Lopez, 548 U.S. 140 (2006). Justice Scalia once stated that, even though he was "a law and order conservative" in his personal views, he should be "a pinup for the criminal defense bar!" David Lat, "Justice Scalia Goes to Wesleyan," *Above the Law,* March 9, 2012, http://abovethelaw.com/2012/03/justice-scalia-goes-to-wesleyan/2/. That was entirely correct, with the single sorry exception of his views concerning the Fifth Amendment privilege against self-incrimination.

5   Brogan v. United States, 522 U.S. 398, 404 (1998).

6   Maryland v. Shatzer, 559 U.S. 98, 108 (2010); Montejo v. Louisiana, 556 U.S. 778, 796 (2009); McNeil v. Wisconsin, 501 U.S. 171, 181 (1991).

7   Mitchell v. United States, 526 U.S. 314, 332 (1999) (dissenting opinion).

8   John H. Blume, "The Dilemma of the Criminal Defendant with a Prior Record—Lessons from the Wrongfully Convicted," *Journal of Empirical Legal Studies* 5, no. 3 (2008): 477, 489–90.

9   Salinas v. Texas, 133 S. Ct. 2174 (2013).

10   "Statement by the President and Attorney General Eric
       Holder," *Whitehouse.gov*, September 25, 2014, https://
       www.whitehouse.gov/the-press-office/2014/09/25
       /statement-president-and-attorney-general-eric-holder.

11   Glossip v. Gross, 135 S. Ct. 2726, 2749 (2015) (concurring
       opinion).

12   Jacob Gershman, "Sotomayor Regales Law School Students
       in Brooklyn," *Wall Street Journal* (April 8, 2016).

13   At the Aspen Ideas Festival in 2013, three years after taking
       her seat on the Supreme Court, former Solicitor General
       Kagan confessed that "the great perk of the job is that I
       haven't been through [airport] security in three years. I
       once had to do it in the last three years, you know, I was on
       personal travel and I didn't inform the Marshals. I couldn't
       remember how, really. It's like, were you supposed to take
       off your shoes?" "Justice Elena Kagan at the Aspen Ideas
       Festival," *YouTube* video, 31:43, from a talk at the Aspen
       Ideas Festival on June 29, 2013, posted by "The Aspen
       Institute," June 29, 2013, https://www.youtube.com
       /watch?v=DC_PVD6YK9g.

14   *Miranda*, 384 U.S. 436, 468 n.37.

15   Berghuis v. Thompkins, 560 U.S. 370 (2010).

16   United States v. Brandt, 546 F.3d 912 (7th Cir. 2008).

17   Debra Cassens Weiss, "Federal Employee Is Indicted for
       Alleged Lies About Confederate Flag Picture in Workplace
       Incident," *ABA Journal*, October 21, 2015.

18   Afraid to take that chance, she more recently pled guilty to

one of the charges, thus reducing her possible prison sentence to five years. Debra Cassens Weiss, "Ex-Federal Worker Faces Possible 5-Year Sentence for Lies about Workplace Confederate Flag Incident," *ABA Journal*, December 28, 2015.

19   Brogan v. United States, 522 U.S. 398, 408 (1998) (concurring opinion).

20   Quin Hillyer, "Ninja Bureaucrats on the Loose: Unfair Laws Are Being Enforced at Gunpoint," *Washington Times*, June 7, 2010; see also George F. Will, "George Will: Blowing the Whistle on Leviathan," *Washington Post*, July 27, 2012; "Armed EPA Raid in Alaska Sheds Light on 70 Fed Agencies with Armed Divisions," *FOX News*, September 14, 2013, http://www.foxnews.com/politics/2013/09/14/armed-epa -agents-in-alaska-shed-light-on-70-fed-agencies-with-armed -divisions.html.

21   John Roberts, "Gibson Guitar Case Drags On with No Sign of Criminal Charges," *FOX News*, April 12, 2012, http:// www.foxnews.com/us/2012/04/12/gibson-guitar-case-drags -on-with-no-sign-criminal-charges.html; Bill Frezza, "Lumber Union Protectionists Incited SWAT Raid on My Factory, Says Gibson Guitar CEO," *Forbes*, May 26, 2014; James R. Hagerty and Kris Maher, "Gibson Guitar Wails on Federal Raid Over Wood," *Wall Street Journal*, September 1, 2011.

22   John R. Emshwiller and Gary Fields, "For Feds, 'Lying' Is a Handy Charge," *Wall Street Journal*, April 9, 2012; see also George F. Will, "George Will: Blowing the Whistle on Leviathan," *Washington Post*, July 27, 2012.

23   United States v. Long, 721 F.3d 920 (8th Cir. 2013).

PART III

1   Maura Dolan, "Boy's Murder Conviction Sharpens Debate on Whether Juveniles Are Fit to Waive Rights," *Los Angeles Times*, November 29, 2015.

2   United States v. Okatan, 728 F.3d 111 (2d Cir. 2013). See also State of Maine v. Lovejoy, 89 A.3d 1066 (2014).

3   Davis v. United States, 512 U.S. 452, 455 (1994) ("Maybe I should talk to a lawyer"); United States v. Younger, 398 F.3d 1179, 1187 (9th Cir. 2005) ("[B]ut, excuse me, if I am right, I can have a lawyer present through all this, right?"); Clark v. Murphy, 331 F.3d 1062, 1065 (9th Cir. 2003) ("I think I would like to talk to a lawyer"); Dormire v. Wilkinson, 249 F.3d 801, 803 (8th Cir. 2001) ("Could I call my lawyer?"); Burket v. Angelone, 208 F.3d 172, 195 (4th Cir. 2000) ("I think I need a lawyer."); United States v. Doe, 170 F.3d 1162, 1166 (9th Cir. 1999) ("What time will I see a lawyer?"); Diaz v. Senkowski, 76 F.3d 61, 63–65 (2d Cir. 1996) ("I think I want a lawyer"); Lord v. Duckworth, 29 F.3d 1216, 1218–21 (7th Cir. 1994) ("I can't afford a lawyer but is there anyway [sic] I can get one?"); United States v. Ogbuehi, 18 F.3d 807, 813–14 (9th Cir. 1994) ("Do you think I need a lawyer?").

4   Sessoms v. Grounds, 776 F.3d 615 (9th Cir. 2015).

ABOUT THE AUTHOR

James J. Duane is a professor at Regent Law School in Virginia Beach, Virginia, where he has received the Faculty Excellence Award three times. Duane has been interviewed about legal matters on television and radio, including National Public Radio's *All Things Considered*, and has testified before the Advisory Committee of the United States Judicial Conference on the Federal Rules of Evidence. He is the coauthor of *Federal Rules of Evidence: Rules, Legislative History, Commentary and Authority* and is a member of the panel of academic contributors to *Black's Law Dictionary*. He is a graduate of Harvard College and the Harvard Law School.